D1566455

North American
P-51 MUSTANG

A Photo Chronicle

Larry Davis

Schiffer Military History
West Chester, PA

Cover Artwork by Steve Ferguson, Colorado Springs, CO

OLD TIGER AND A NEW PONY

The P-51B Mustang illustrated as "DING HAO" (Good Luck) flown by former Flying Tiger ace and eventual 356th FS CO Major Jim Howard. Although "DING HAO" has the typical white I.D. markings of USAAF ETO single-seat fighters, the white paint on the nose does not extend back to the exhaust ports, as was standard on the Mustangs in the following months. "DING HAO" has three reversed swastikas below the windscreen and would later display Howard's total of six Japanese and seven German victories.

The major led his own men on the famous escort mission of 11 January 1944, to strike the Third Reich's Halberstadt and Oschersleben aircraft factories. While temporarily separated from his squadron, the China ace single-handedly held off over thirty enemy aircraft in several different encounters and shot down four of the Luftwaffe interceptors. For his extraordinary skill and bravery, Howard was awarded the Medal of Honor, one of only two fighter pilots in the European theater to receive the decoration.

Rear Cover Top:
A group of fighter-bomber pilots pose in front of an A-36A at the Florida AAF training base near Orlando in 1943. *(via Dick Starinchak)*

Rear Cover Bottom:
"The Iowa Beaut", the P-51B flown by Lt. Lee Mendenhall with the 354th FS/355th FG showing 10 victories. *(USAF)*

Book Design by Robert Biondi

Copyright © 1992 by Larry Davis.
Library of Congress Catalog Number: 92-81714

Printed in the United States of America.
ISBN: 0-88740-411-1

We are interested in hearing from authors with book ideas on related topics.

Published by Schiffer Publishing Ltd.
1469 Morstein Rd.
West Chester, PA 19380
Please write for a free catalog.
This book may be purchased from the publisher.
Please include $2.95 postage.
Try your bookstore first.

Contents

Introduction

MUSTANG – considered by many to be the finest fighter aircraft design of all time. Perhaps, but at the very least it was most certainly the finest during the era of World War II. No, the Mustang was not the best aircraft in every performance category. In fact the Mustang was rarely THE best in any category. The Lockheed P-38 Lightning had a greater range; the Supermarine Spitfire was more maneuverable; the Republic P-47 Thunderbolt could outdive it and was more heavily armed, and the DeHavilland Mosquito was faster. However, the Mustang could not only perform almost equal to any aircraft in each of the performance categories, the Mustang was easily better than any adversary, friendly or enemy, in ALL the categories combined. It was simply the best OVERALL fighter design of the war. How did the Mustang evolve into the ultimate fighter design? It certainly did not start out that way. But let's start at the very beginning.

•

One would be hard pressed to rationalize how a small company that simply held interests in a wide variety of aviation companies, would evolve into the biggest producer of military aircraft in the entire world for the next two decades. Not only as the most prolific, North American Aviation would hold title to the best trainer aircraft – the T-6 Texan, the best fighter aircraft in World War II – the Mustang, the best jet fighter of the post-war period – the F-86 Sabre, and the first operational jet fighter to break the sound barrier in level flight – the F-100 Super Sabre. And that's not counting the B-25 Mitchell, a very good medium bomber in World War II, or the FJ Fury carrier launched jet fighter series, nor the fantastic X-15 rocket plane. All were North American designs.

North American Aviation began as a holding company in 1928, with Clement Keys at the head. Keys had investments in almost every facet of aviation during the era including Curtiss Aeroplane and Motor Co., Transcontinental Air Transport (which evolved into TWA), Douglas Aircraft, and Atlantic Aircraft Corp., license builder of both Fokker tri-motor transport aircraft and DeHavilland DH-4 observation aircraft. In 1929 General Motors Corp. acquired the Atlantic Aircraft Corp. and changed the name to General Aviation. In 1932 GM purchased additional stock from Keys and renamed the company North American Aviation Inc. However, the company remained only a licensee to build Fokker designs.

In 1934 two things occurred which would change the course of history for North American Aviation forever.

NAA engineer Louis Wait checks the NA-73 wind tunnel model at Ames research center. *(NAA)*

The brain trust at North American Aviation, (left to right) Lee Atwood, "Dutch" Kindelberger, and Stan Smithson check the final drawings of their new design. *(NAA)*

Seven years later these changes would affect the outcome of mankinds greatest struggle. First, the Douglas Aircraft Company developed the DC-1/DC-2 airliner design, an aircraft that totally revolutionized the air transport business. The success of the Douglas design meant that no one wanted the obsolete Fokker designs anymore and North American Aviation no longer had any airplanes to build. Second, Ernest Breech, Chairman of the Board of North American, decided to completely reorganize the fledgling company under the leadership of James H. "Dutch" Kindelberger. Dutch foresaw a company that would design AND build their own aircraft. No longer would North American build anothers designs. Dutch also knew that the sales market lay with the military. Dutch's first move to bring the company into the forefront of aviation was to move the company, lock, stock, and barrel, including all eighty-five employees, to a new plant in Inglewood, California. America's west coast was the hotbed of aviation – and remains so today.

The new company's first successful venture into the military aircraft field was North American design 16 or NA-16, military designation Basic Trainer type 9 or BT-9. The basic design of the BT-9 would ultimately evolve into the worlds best known trainer aircraft of all time – the renowned North American T-6 Texan. The Texan (aka the SNJ by the Navy), and Harvard with the RAF/RCAF, would be built in more numbers, and flown by air forces of more nations than almost every fighter aircraft it would train pilots for. The Texan had enough performance that it was a natural to develop into an inexpensive fighter aircraft. The NA-50/NA-68 was basically an armed, single-seat fighter based extensively on BT-9/T-6 technology. How-

The Mustang design team – (left to right) Louis Wait, Ray Rice, and Edgar Schmued, the Chief Design Engineer for the project. *(NAA)*

ever, the performance simply was not on a par with the contemporary fighter designs of the era such as the Curtiss P-40 and Lockheed P-38. North American did sell seven NA-50s to Peru, and six NA-68s to the Siam Air

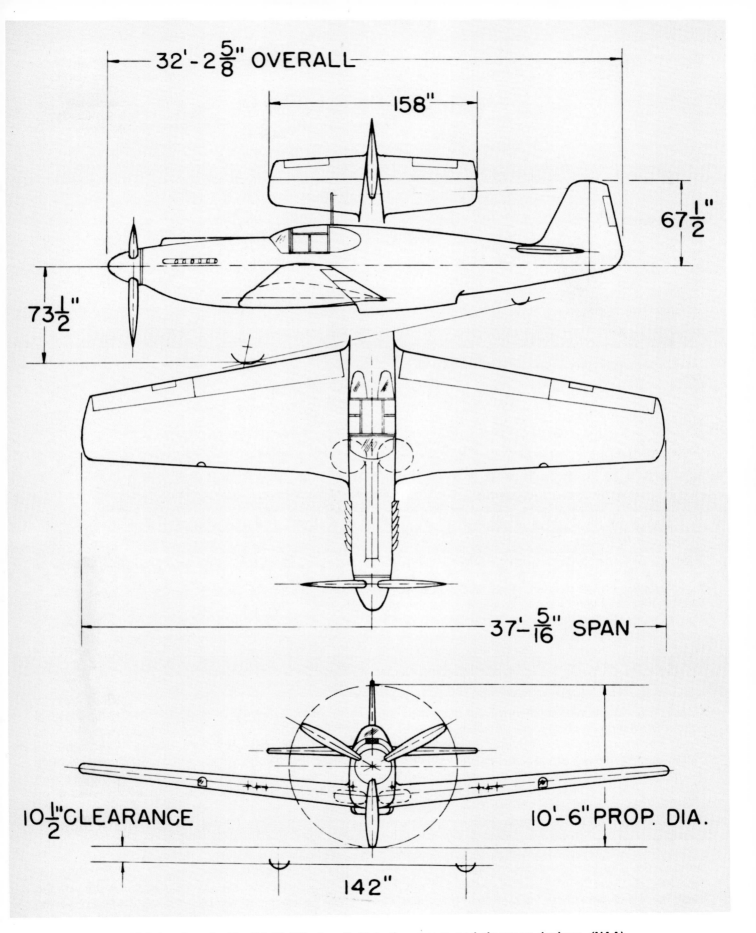

Initial drawings for the NA-73-OO aircraft. Note the canopy and air scoop designs. *(NAA)*

Dick Schleicher, Chief Structural Engineer (dark suit), conducts the wing loading tests on the NA-73X as Ray Rice, Lee Atwood, and Edgar Schmued recheck the drawings. *(NAA)*

Force in 1940 making the company's first venture into the fighter aircraft field somewhat of a success.

In the Spring of 1940, the British Royal Air Force was already involved in heavy air fighting with the German Luftwaffe. British air officers realized that manufacturing capabilities in England would be sorely taxed to meet the needs for fighter aircraft to defeat the Germans. They began to look elsewhere for modern aircraft. The elsewhere that they looked was west in the Colonies. American fighters weren't the best aircraft in the world, but they could hold their own, especially in the role of ground attack and bombing aircraft. One of the aircraft designs chosen was the Curtiss P-40 Tomahawk. If American P-40s could be bought in sufficient quantities, it would free the English manufacturers to build the superb Spitfires that were needed to keep the skies over England clear of German bombers. But Curtiss Aircraft Co. was already manufacturing P-40s at maximum capacity for US Army use. The British Air Purchasing Commission sought a second

company that could license-build the P-40 for RAF use. In early 1940 the BAPC contacted North American Aviation officials about just such a project.

After reviewing both the BAPC request and the actual needs of the RAF, Dutch Kindelberger and his top assistant John Leland "Lee" Atwood, proposed that North American be allowed to develop its own design. It would be the seventy third North American design proposal, more commonly known as NA-73. Design specifications for a high performance fighter of the type needed had been in the works at North American since mid-1939. It was a simple thing for Lee Atwood to modify them to meet the British requirements. On 24 April 1940, the BAPC approved the basic design sketches. Within a month the NA-73 design was approved for sale to the RAF by the US government. And on 29 May the RAF ordered 320 of the new aircraft based solely on the drawings and projected performance. The US Army Air Corps had no interest in the design at this time. In conjunction with the order, the

Rollout of the NA-73X took place on 9 September 1940, minus its engine and equipped with main wheels and tires from one of North American's BC-1 trainer aircraft. This photo was taken later after the engine was installed. *(NAA)*

Vance Breese (hands behind back) listens to the NAA engineers as the mechanics ready the NA-73X for its first flight on 26 October 1940. *(NAA)*

RAF came up with a name that would refer to the aircraft forevermore. The name chosen was MUSTANG.

With a basic design sketch and the specifications list in hand, the North American design team set to their task. The task seemed very formidable, made especially so as there was a 120 day time limit in which North American had to bring the NA-73 from rough sketch to prototype rollout. But the design team was equal to the task. Led by Dutch Kindelberger, a world-class stressed-skin aircraft engineer, the NA-73 design team consisted of Lee Atwood, Vice President of NAA and a former structural engineer with Douglas Aircraft Co.; Raymond Rice, NAA Chief Engineer, had been a structural engineer with the Martin Aircraft Co.; Edgar Schmued, a Bavarian-born/German schooled aeronautical engineer was named Chief Design Engineer; Project Engineer was Herb Baldwin, another ex-Douglas employee; while Ed Horkey, fresh out of college, would be in charge of the aerodynamics of the aircraft. It was Edgar Schmued's sketches that the BAPC had approved. Schmued's basic design, with two major exceptions, would remain unaltered throughout the production run.

Schmued's design for the NA-73 called for an all-metal, stressed-skin monoplane. It was to be powered by the tried and proven Allison V-1710, 12 cylinder, liquid-cooled, inline V-12 engine. The engine, with a single speed, single stage supercharger, offered 1120 hp at 3000 rpm. However, the chosen version of the V-1710 was the -39, whose horsepower peaked at about 13,000 feet altitude. Performance fell off rapidly above this altitude. Maximum speed was estimated to be over 375 mph, about 25 mph faster than the Spitfire V. The engine mount was another innovation from Schmued – a pair of aluminum beams as opposed to the normal practice of using sheet steel tubing for the engine mount. Not only would the mounts hold the engine, they would also serve as mounts for a pair of .50 caliber machine guns in the nose of the aircraft.

Ed Horkey developed the radiator location and design. Contemporary European design such as the Spitfire and the Messerschmitt Bf 109, had the glycol and oil cooler radiators mounted under the wings, while American designs like the P-40 and P-38 had their radiators located under the nose. Both radiator locations were the cause of a great deal of added drag on the airframe. Drag that had to be overcome with horsepower. Horkey used some Curtiss technology derived from the XP-46 and developed a radiator that used a location on the underside of the fuselage aft of the wing trailing edge. Schmued and Horkey came up with a radiator design that not only combined both the glycol and supercharger oil coolers in one heat exchanger, but one that had a very low drag factor. Additionally, and completely by accident, it was

found that the radiator design actually provided about 300 lbs. of jet thrust similar to a ramjet.

The wing of the NA-73 was what really made the design fly – no pun intended. The wing was a radical new design proposed by A.C. Robinson of the National Advisory Committee for Aeronautics, which held great promise for high performance aircraft. It was known as a LAMINAR FLOW wing. On a normal wing design, the wing is at its thickest near the leading edge. This results in a loss of boundary layer adhesion at high speeds and a turbulent air flow over the rest of the wing. And turbulence creates drag. With a laminar flow design, the wing was thin at the leading edge, with the thickest portion of the wing moved as near to the trailing edge as possible. This allowed the boundary layer airflow to retain its adhesion to the wing for longer periods of time, thus maintaining a much smoother flow of air over the remainder of the wing. Turbulence was reduced and consequently drag was also reduced. On the NA-73 both the upper and lower wing plans were of the laminar flow design, being almost symmetrical in shape.

Another very critical matter was that the laminar flow wing had to be as smooth as possible from leading edge to control surfaces. Previous experiments with the laminar flow design had used hand-built wings of exact tolerances, many made from highly polished wood. But a military airplane in mass production could hardly have wings that had to be hand-made, one at a time. North American proposed a tight-tolerance wing design, but one that was easily mass-produced. The wing would be flush-riveted and all the seams would be filled, sanded, and painted at the factory. With this concept, all the production Mustang aircraft had both the upper and lower wing surfaces filled, sanded, and painted for a completely smooth air flow. Even the later so-called "natural metal"

Vance Breese at the controls of the NA-73X during the first flight. It carries the civil registration NX 19998. Note the short upper carburetor scoop and round, one-piece windscreen. *(NAA)*

NAA Test Pilot Paul Balfour was at the controls of the NA-73X when an engine problem caused the aircraft to lose all power and crash in a field west of the plant. The NA-73X was repaired and flew many more test flights before being retired on 15 July 1941. *(NAA)*

Mustangs had silver painted wings from the factory.

The laminar flow wing design also allowed for carriage of fuel, weapons, and landing gear within the wing. The landing gear retracted into the inner wing. One unusual feature was that the main landing gear doors remained closed except during the actual retraction cycle, thus retaining a smooth air flow under the wing and into the radiator intake. The tail wheel was also retractable and covered by doors. Within the wing were a pair of 85 gallon fuel tanks. And just outboard of the fuel tanks and main landing gear bays were the weapon and ammunition compartments. Weapons varied within the many different Mustang production variants, but the NA-73 was designed around the British-specified armament of two .30 caliber machine guns flanking a single .50 caliber gun in each wing, with another pair of .50 caliber guns in the nose.

On 9 September 1940, the completed airframe was rolled out of the Inglewood plant – minus engine. It had taken the NAA engineers and craftsmen 102 days to build the prototype aircraft, which was designated the NA-73X. Since the aircraft was to be powered by the venerable Allison V-1710, and was merely a prototype project not even slated for use by the US Army, the NA-73X had to take a back seat on the priority list to the Curtiss P-40 already in production. All the available Allison engines were slated for P-40 production. On 7 October 1940, one of the big Allison V-12s arrived at the Inglewood plant. Within four days, the engine was installed, wired, and made ready for flight. On 11 October 1940, the Allison coughed into life for the first time. Ground tests of all the aircraft systems began immediately.

Over the next fifteen days each system was checked and rechecked. Taxi and brake tests were conducted. Finally, on the morning of 26 October 1940, the NA-73X was deemed ready for flight. Vance Breese taxied the gleaming silver aircraft to the end of the runway at Mines Field, now the site of Los Angeles International Airport. Every member of the 97 man NA-73X team that could

make it was there to watch the historic occasion. Breese closed and locked the cockpit hatch cover, adjusted the throttle for takeoff, made a final check of his instruments, and released the brakes. The NA-73X leapt forward, the tail lifted, the main wheels lifted, and Breese and the NA-73X were airborne. He cycled the landing gear and began the required initial tests. Twenty minutes later Breese touched down again at Mines Field and taxied to a stop in front of the North American crowd. Breese was ecstatic! The NA-73X had not only performed all the initial tests required, it had far exceeded all the requirements. The NAA engineering crew was excited, the visiting RAF officials were excited, even the US Army Air Corps representative was excited.

Following eight uneventful but highly successful test flights with Breese at the controls, NAA turned the aircraft over to Paul Balfour, another test pilot. Balfour flew an airspeed calibration flight on 20 November which ended in disaster. Twelve minutes into the flight the big Allison simply stopped. Balfour tried everything he could think of but the engine remained still. Balfour was only 250 feet above the ground but he was out of range to make the runway. He lowered the landing gear and flaps and put the NA-73X down in a farmers field just east of the Mines runway. When the landing gear encountered the freshly plowed earth, the NA-73X stopped almost instantly, flipping over onto its back. Although Balfour was unhurt, the NA-73X was extensively damaged and it was thought it would never fly again. The cause of the problem was a simple one but one that took some thought to solve. The engine was starved for fuel. The problem was the short carburetor intake causing the engine to stall. Eventually the scoop was lengthened and the problem was solved. Although often thought to be destroyed in this crash, North American Aviation records show that the NA-73X was repaired and flew an additional 36 flights after the crash. The NA-73X was officially retired on 15 July 1941.

Production

Mustang production began in early 1941 with the British Air Purchasing Committee order for 320 aircraft that was placed in August 1940. The first Mustang I, RAF serial AG 345, rolled off the Inglewood assembly line on 16 April 1941. After seven days of ground tests, Vance Breese took AG 345 into the air for the first time. The aircraft was virtually identical to the prototype NA-73X. The aircraft was not camouflaged nor fitted with armament of any type. All the gun openings were faired over. The only exterior difference between AG-345 and the NA-73X was the use of a new three-piece windshield with a flat center panel. AG-345 remained at Inglewood as a North American test aircraft throughout the remainder of its service life.

The second aircraft, AG 346, was the first to carry the RAF prescribed camouflage and armament. In the nose under the exhaust were a pair of additional .50 caliber guns. After the required taxi and flight tests at Inglewood, AG 346 was disassembled, crated, and shipped to England. Arriving at Liverpool, AG 346 was reassembled and fitted with some of the normal RAF flight gear such as RAF radios, gunsight, and the circular handgrip on the control column. The first flight in England took place in early November from nearby RAF Burtonwood. The results took everyone by surprise – especially the RAF officials in attendance.

The tests revealed a top speed of 382 mph as compared to the 390 mph of the NA-73X prototype. Considering the additional weight of the eight machine guns and ammunition, plus the required RAF radio gear, and a couple of hundred pounds in camouflage paint, the speed was well within tolerable limits. Up to 15,000 feet altitude the Mustang I was some 45 mph faster than the best RAF fighter then in use, the Spitfire V. RAF aircrew exclaimed that the ground handling characteristics were better than any other aircraft. This was due to the 12' wheel track of the main landing gear. Tests revealed the problem with the carburation which was cured by enlarging the carburetor air intake and lengthening the scoop, bringing it even with the propeller hub/forward fuselage line. This was the same problem that had almost cost the life of Paul Balfour in the NA-73X. The extended carburetor scoop was incorporated on all Allison-engined Mustangs beginning with the third production aircraft.

However, all the tests did not result in phenomenal success. The performance of the Mustang I fell off so badly above 15,000' that the RAF ordered the aircraft into its ground attack squadrons to supplement the Curtiss P-40 Tomahawks already in service. The Mustang I would also perform the photo recon mission for the RAF, at least

AG 345 was the first production aircraft, now named Mustang I. It differed from the prototype in having British "combat equipment" and a three piece windscreen. (NAA)

the low level tactical missions. For the photo recon mission a pair of F-24 cameras were mounted in the fuselage; one directly behind the pilot and aimed out through the left rear side glass; a second camera could be mounted in the bottom of the fuselage immediately behind the forward radiator door.

The first unit to be fully operational in the Mustang I was No. 2 Squadron in January 1942. But testing, pilot and ground crew training, plus the factory and RAF mandated modifications, held up the combat introduction of the aircraft. By May 1942 2 Sq was declared combat operational and the unit flew its first mission on 19 May 1942, a strafing mission to Berch sur Mer airdrome in France. F/O G. N. Dawson also caught a German train out in the open and shot it to pieces. On 27 July 1942, the RAF Mustang Is did something that no other fighter aircraft was capable of doing. They flew a fighter sweep from their bases in England and attacked targets inside Germany. It was just a hint of what was to come.

On 19 August 1942, the total number of Mustang I squadrons in the RAF stood at four, all of which were part of the force operating against the Germans during the ill-fated Dieppe Raid. Although the raid was a disaster of the first magnitude, the Mustang was bloodied for the first time. During the first days operations, 414 Sq, RCAF, encountered several flights of German Fw 190 fighters. F/O Hollis Hills, an American volunteer with the RCAF whose home was only a few miles from the North American plant in Pasadena, became the first Mustang pilot to achieve a victory over an enemy aircraft when he shot down one of the Fw 190s. However, the Luftwaffe also

scored a first when an Fw 190 pilot shot down a Mustang. It was the first, but definitely not the last, in either category.

Although initially the US Army had expressed little interest in the new North American fighter designed to British specs, the results of tests on the NA-73X and Mustang I quickly brought a complete turnaround in their attitude. With its first flight, this little fighter designed to meet a foreign air force requirement, made obsolete all but one aircraft type then in service with the US Army Air Force. The only aircraft that could exceed the test results of the NA-73X was the Lockheed P-38 Lightning. And that advantage too would soon fall.

The Army Air Force took delivery of the 4th and 10th Mustang Is off the Inglewood assembly line. They were designated XP-51, Army serial numbers 41-038 and -039, and delivered to Wright Field for tests on 24 August and 16 December 1941 respectively. But Army priorities at Wright Field on aircraft types slated for US procurement found 41-038 being placed into storage immediately. An experimental pneumatic gun charger contract sent the XP-51 to Eglin Field to begin tests. The XP-51 was chosen for the joint RAF/US Navy test program on the gun charger simply because it was available. The Army had no plans for the XP-51 at the time and the gun charger tests had a high priority. But when the test pilots came back from the gun charger tests extolling the flight performance of the XP-51, the Army brass decided to take a closer look at the aircraft. After reading all the enthusiastic pilot reports from Eglin, Army sent -038 to Langley Field for extensive NACA testing that began on 1 March 1942.

The production P-51 aircraft differed greatly from

their RAF counterparts. The extended carburetor airscoop was incorporated, but RAF mandated armament and radio requirements were changed. The pair of .50 caliber guns in the nose were deleted entirely. The wing armament was changed to two Hispano-Suiza 20mm cannon in each wing. The radiator intake was slightly altered, as were the aileron controls. The US Army had ordered 150 Mustang Is for Lend Lease to the RAF. It was from this initial order that Army began filling its inventories with P-51s, named Apache by Army officials. The RAF also took delivery of some of the 20mm armed aircraft, designating them as Mustang Ia. Of the original order for 150 Mustang I aircraft, 93 went to RAF units where they served in the ground support role; while 57 P-51 Apaches went to US Army Air Force units.

The US Army Air Force mission for the P-51 was that of photo reconnaissance. The great performance of the aircraft below 15,000' made the P-51 ideal in this role. North American modified 55 of the 57 P-51s with the addition of two US Army K-24 cameras mounted in the same position as their RAF counterparts. Officially designated F-6A, the units operating the aircraft simply referred to them as P-51s since they retained their 20mm cannon armament. The first US Army unit equipped with the P-51/F-6A was the 7th Photo Group, assigned to the Photo recon training school at Peterson Field, Colorado. Following introduction into Army service, the name MUSTANG was officially adopted for both RAF and USAAF aircraft.

At about the time that US Army was forming its initial Mustang units, the RAF was about to crown the first Mustang Ace. It was the same American volunteer that had scored the first Mustang victory on 19 August 1942. Now promoted to Flight Lieutenant, Hollis Hills scored his fifth victory on 11 June 1943. Following Operation "Torch", the Allied landings on the west coast of Africa, and being heavily involved in the subsequent defeat of the Afrika Korps, many Army Air Force units began operations against Hitler's Festung Europa from bases in North Africa. One of these was the first US Army combat operational unit flying P-51s, the 154th Observation Squadron equipped with P-51/F-6A Mustangs. Based at Sbeitla Airdrome in French Morocco, Lt. Alfred Schwab flew the first US Mustang combat mission on 9 April 1943, when he photographed the Luftwaffe airfield at Kairouan. The North African campaign also pointed up the disastrous similarity in appearance between the Mustang and German Bf 109. On 23 April 1943, Army anti-aircraft gunners shot down a 154th OS P-51, which they mistakenly took to be a Bf 109 at speed. Soon after this, all Mustangs had broad Yellow bands painted on the vertical and horizontal tail surfaces to allow quick recognition of the aircraft.

The first US Army order for the Mustang was the direct result of General Hap Arnold. But Hap didn't want the aircraft as either a fighter nor a photo recce aircraft. General Arnold recognized (a) the performance capabilities of the Mustang from the Eglin/Langley test results; and (b) the Army Air Force need for a high performance, low level

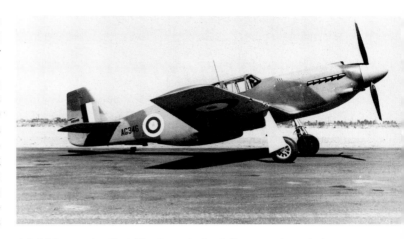

AG 346 was the first Mustang to be fully armed, and also to wear camouflage paint – called for in the British requirements. *(NAA)*

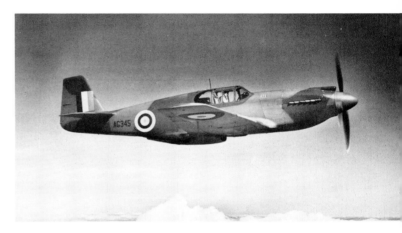

AG 345, now in RAF camouflage and having the longer carburetor intake scoop, flew most of the initial Mustang flight test program while NA-73X was being repaired. *(NAA)*

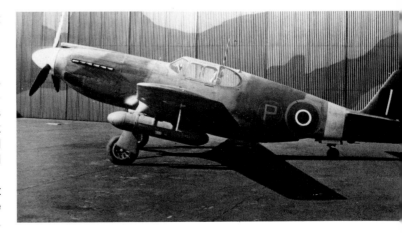

A large yellow "P" for Prototype adorns the side of AM 106 on the ramp at RAF Boscombe Down, the RAF test facility. *(R.L. Ward)*

ground attack aircraft. An order was placed with North American on 16 April 1942 for 500 Mustang Is modified for the ground attack mission. The aircraft were designated A-36A. The A-36A differed from the Mustang I/P-51/F-6A in armament and flight controls. The Army requirement called for an armament of four .50 caliber guns in the wings, with an additional pair of .50s in the nose. Also, the A-36 wing was modified to include an upper and lower dive "brake" that would keep the dive speed low enough to allow accurate aiming. These dive "brakes" were cast aluminum slabs, slotted to allow some airflow that were hydraulically extended into the airstream above and below the wing, thus limiting the air speed to 390 mph. This dive "brake" concept had been borrowed from the similarly equipped Vultee A-31 Vengeance dive bomber.

But wait! How could the A-36 carry bombs. No Mustang had any provision for carrying ordnance either internally or externally. The development of the underwing bomb rack would lead to a much more significant event. Actually the carriage of bombs was an afterthought. With the German U-boat fleet roaming the Atlantic at will, and sinking everything in their sights, Army Air Force decided to try ferry flights to get the combat aircraft to England. Although the range of the Mustang I was extensive, 900 miles, it still was outside the scope of a trans-Atlantic crossing. Army and North American came up with an idea to fit a B-7 bomb shackle under each wing outboard of the landing gear. By mounting standard 75 gallon jettisonable fuel tanks on the B-7 shackles, the ferry range of the

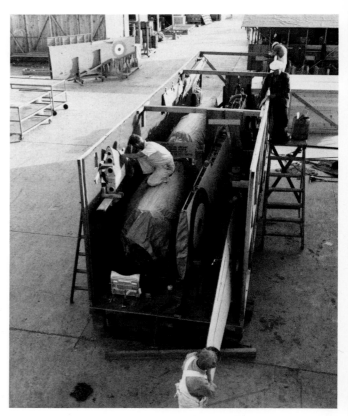

Following initial factory flight tests and BAPC acceptance, the first Mustang Is were disassembled and crated for shipment to England. *(NAA)*

A NAA technician in England backs one of the brand new Mustang Is into a revetment at Burtonwood Assembly Area in 1942. *(NAA)*

A Mustang I from RAF 26 Squadron over England in August 1942, carries an F-24 camera aft of the cockpit. RAF Mustang Is were armed with two .30 caliber machine guns and one .50 caliber gun in each wing, plus two .50s in the nose. *(via R.L. Ward)*

Proof that the Mustang I could take it is seen with this riddled RCAF 414 Squadron aircraft hit over Holland in the late summer of 1944. *(M. Robinson via R.L. Ward)*

The first US Army Air Force production aircraft was the P-51, nick-named Apache, armed with four 20mm cannon instead of the RAF machine gun requirement. *(NAA)*

Most of the AAF P-51s were fitted with K-24 cameras and used for the photo reconnaissance mission. *(AFM)*

Mustang grew to 1600 miles; and Lockheed designed 165 gallon tanks (for the P-38) increased the range to 2500 miles. Once in the combat theater, the drop tanks could be exchanged for 500 lb. bombs. Thus a requirement for longer range to avoid the U-boat attacks led to a successful fighter bomber aircraft capable of delivering 1000 lbs. of ordnance at high speed. And later led to fighter escort missions throughout Germany.

Other changes in the A-36A included a repositioning of the landing light and pitot boom due to the dive brake installation. The powerplant was changed to the V-1710-87 that offered 1325 hp at 3000' for the ground attack mission. US Army designated the aircraft A-36A-1NA and named it INVADER. First flight of an A-36A took place on 21 September 1942. Performance of the Invader was down from that of the Mustang fighter due to the added weight of the dive brake systems, and the plumbing and wiring for the B-7 shackle installation. Airspeed was down from 382 mph to 368 mph at 14,000', but speed increased from 328mph to 366 mph at 1000.'

In April 1943, the 27th Fighter Bomber Group was in place in French Morocco. After reassembly and testing at Rasel Ma, the 27th FBG flew the first A-36 missions on 6 June 1943. The A-36As supported the invasion of Pantelleria Island. The island was captured almost from the use of air power alone. By 20 June the 27th and 86th FBGs were flying missions from the captured airfields. Flying from Pantelleria, the A-36s pounded Sicilian targets with over 1000 sorties per day during the campaign to liberate the island. Only one other Army unit was equipped with the A-36A, the 311th FBG at Dinjan, India. The 311th FBG supported the defense of the Ledo Road in Burma.

Army statistics show that the three groups of A-36s flew 23,373 combat sorties, dropping 8,014 tons of bombs, shot down 84 enemy aircraft in the air and a further 17 on the ground, while losing 177 of their own in the toughest mission of them all – low level ground support.

The last version of the Allison-powered Mustang was the P-51A, RAF Mustang II. The P-51A was developed concurrently with the A-36A. Originally the P-51A was to be a P-51/Mustang I using the new, more efficient V-1710-81 engine. The -81 had a new supercharger, propeller, and combined with an overall lighter weight, increased both the top speed and rate of climb. With a new Curtiss 10'9" propeller, the rate of climb rose to 3800 feet/minute. Deletion of the two nose guns and the dive brakes reduced the aircraft weight by 750 lbs. The top speed rose to 409 mph at 10,000.' Ferry range with the Lockheed 165 gallon tanks installed rose to 2740 miles.

A contract with Army on 23 June 1942 meant a production run of 1200 P-51As. However, this was reduced in December 1942 to 310 aircraft. Of these, 50 went to Great Britain to replace the 57 Mustang Is diverted from Lend Lease contract to US Army use. Of the remaining 260 aircraft, 35 had the two K-24 camera installations added as on the F-6A, and were designated F-6B. The first flight of a P-51A took place on 3 February 1943, and production aircraft deliveries began in March.

The first unit to take delivery of the P-51A was the veteran 311th FBG in India during the summer of 1943. Already equipped with the A-36A, the 311th would be equipped with two squadrons of P-51As and one overstrength squadron of A-36As. Next unit to convert was the 23rd Fighter Group, the Flying Tigers based at

Kweilin, China. The Flying Tigers traded in their beloved and very war-weary P-40 Warhawks for Mustangs in September 1943. They would be the first unit to fly what has universally become known as the role the Mustang was developed for – the bomber escort mission. On 25 November 1943, Thanksgiving Day, the 23rd took 8 P-51As and 8 P-38Gs and flew escort on a B-25 force attacking the airfield at Shinchiku, Formosa. By the end of 1943, P-51As equipped three Groups in the China/Burma/India Theater, as well as several recon squadrons and RAF units in North Africa.

When the final P-51A rolled off the Inglewood assembly line, it brought total production of the Allison-powered Mustang to 1570 aircraft. The RAF purchased or obtained through Lend Lease, 764 Mustang I, Mustang Ia, and Mustang II aircraft. Ten of these were sold to the Soviet Union for tests in anticipation of a contract with that nation that never materialized.

The Mustang had arrived! The Mustang was already the premier fighter-bomber aircraft in the war, packing enough punch to deliver 1000 lbs of ordnance throughout any of the war theaters. And it still had enough to mix it up with the Axis fighters – if they chose to come down to fight. The next development would allow the Mustang pilots to go UP after the Axis fighters, and would result in the Mustang becoming the best overall fighter aircraft of World War II, from any nation, in any theater, for any mission!

One AAF P-51 had an elaborate black and white zebra-stripe paint scheme. It was thought the stripes would disrupt enemy gunners, but did not prove out. The stripes were only carried on the fuselage sides and underside of the aircraft. *(USAF)*

"Betty Jean", a P-51 from the 111th Tactical Recon Squadron/68th Observation Group, taxis into a wine barrel and sandbag Anzio beachhead revetment on 6 April 1944. Cockpit visibility was poor in the P-51 and ground crewmen rode on the wing to direct the pilot. *(USAF)*

A P-51 from the 111th TRS/68th TRG on the ramp at Santa Maria, Italy during the summer of 1944. *(Don Garrett Jr.)*

Captain Dave Harrell stands beside his P-51, also designated F-6A, at Santa Maria Airfield in Italy. The 111th TRS was an activated Texas Air Guard squadron known as the "Snoopers." *(USAF)*

A trio of A-36A "Invaders" over Southern California in 1943. With its high speed and durability, the A-36A was the best AAF dive bomber until replaced by P-47 Thunderbolts. *(NAA)*

A North American technician stands by with the fire extinguisher during engine run-up tests on an A-36. Armament again was changed on the A-36A, now having four .50s in the wings and two more .50s in the nose. *(NAA)*

An A-36A from the 526th FBS/86 FG at Tafaraoui, Algeria in 1943, showing 80+ mission markers from the nose to the tail. *(Merle Olmsted)*

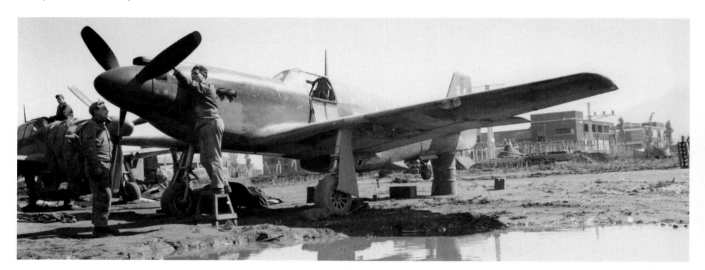

This A-36A from the 86th FG crashed at Gela, Sicily in 1943 and was put back into service. AAF ground crews worked many miracles throughout the war in keeping the aircraft flying. *(USAF)*

A red-nosed A-36A from the 86th FG taxis past a group of RAF Baltimores at Gela, Sicily. The yellow band around the wing was a quick ID device as the Mustang was similar in outline to the Messerschmitt Bf 109. *(Robert Esposito)*

A bombed-up 527th FBS A-36A showing 150 mission marks poses with the ground crew at Ciampino, Italy in the Spring of 1944. After 150 missions, the only damage suffered was a flak hit to the left aileron. *(USAF)*

"Margie H" is the sole remaining A-36A known to exist today. "Margie" was restored by the Minnesota Air National Guard, complete with the full combat markings it carried when it served with the 522nd FBS in North Africa. The A-36A now resides in the Air Force Museum at Dayton, Ohio. *(NAA)*

The P-51A was quite similar to the A-36A but minus the wing dive brakes and the nose machine gun armament. *(NAA)*

"Mrs. Virginia" shows some very heavy exhaust stains as it flies wing to the 1st Air Commando Group CO, Colonel Phil Cochran. The extreme long range of China missions called for installation of a direction-finder loop antenna atop the rear fuselage. *(USAF)*

The P-51As from the 530th FS/311th FG were some of the first to fly long range, bomber escort mission when they used 75 gallon drop tanks on a B-25 escort mission to Formosa in November 1943. *(USAF)*

P-51As from the 1st ACG lined up at Broadway Field in Burma. Most of the P-51A production run went to units in the China/Burma/India Theater. *(USAF)*

Major James England shot down eight Japanese fighters while serving as the CO of the 530th FS at Dinjan in 1944. *(USAF)*

P-51As were also used in the fighter-bomber role in China. This 311th FG P-51A carries a pair of 500 lb. bombs and has been fitted with underwing "bazooka" rocket launchers. *(USAF)*

Mechanics perform some minor engine adjustments to Major John England's P-51A at Dinjan, India in 1944. Open-air maintenance, in monsoon rains or tropical heat, was the norm in the CBI Theater. *(USAF)*

"Jeanie" was an F-6B (P-51A) flown by Lt. Keating with 32 photo missions. "Jeanie" was assigned to the 107th TRS/67th TRG at LeMolay Airdrome, France in the Summer of 1944. *(Fred LePage)*

The Merlin Engine

Why was it necessary to put the Rolls-Royce Merlin into the Mustang? Why didn't AAF, North American, and Allison simply develop the V-1710 that was already in use in the P-40 and P-51? The power was available from the Allison, but the time wasn't! In 1942 the Allison was still many months away from its full potential. Months that the Allied Powers did not have. The RAF, USAAF, and North American all realized the need for a higher altitude-rated, high performance engine to fit the P-51 airframe that wind tunnel tests had shown to be the most aerodynamically efficient fighter design in history. Enter the Rolls-Royce Merlin and its license-built cousin, the Packard Merlin.

Development of the Merlin engine began in 1925 when Rolls-Royce produced the first aluminum block V-12 engine. The cylinders had steel sleeves for the piston bores. The head was a radical design that incorporated four valves per cylinder. The supercharged KESTRAL engine developed 745 hp at 14,599 ft. altitude. A later development known as the "R" engine produced 1900 hp. This engine and a subsequent development that produced 2530 hp, were the engines that powered the Supermarine S-6 racing seaplane to the World Speed Record of 407.5 mph, and a Schneider Cup victory in 1929. 407.5 mph in 1929! In a seaplane! The S-6 was certainly a clean design for a seaplane, but it still had those huge floats hanging out into the slipstream creating drag. And drag could only be overcome by horsepower. It was the tremendous potential of the radical Rolls-Royce engine that allowed the S-6 to be successful. The "R" engine not only developed a fantastic amount of horsepower, it could also turn over 1000 rpm faster than any competing engine type and handle an additional 100 psi BMEP, or manifold torque pressure. All of this gave a much greater power range to the "R" engine.

The key to all the additional horsepower was in the supercharger. It was a two stage, two speed design, offering a 4:1 boost ratio. Fuel was injected directly into the supercharger through a radical new induction system developed by the Stromberg Carburetor Division of Bendix Aviation. By the early 1940s all the bugs had been worked out of the Rolls-Royce engine, something the Allison V-1710 still had to conquer. Both the Hawker Hurricane and Supermarine Spitfire used Merlin engines. And their record against the vaunted German Luftwaffe in the Battle of Britain speaks for itself.

The great need for Merlin engines, not only to power the Spitfire and Hurricane but also the Lancaster and Wellington bombers, led to a licensing agreement between

Night firing tests and bore-sighting of the four .50 caliber guns. Although the armament was effective, the canted gun installation was prone to jamming and considered light in hitting power when compared to the P-47. *(NAA)*

The Mustang X aircraft was derived from mating a production Mustang I airframe and the Merlin engine. The deep chin carburetor intake was found only on the Mustang X aircraft. *(Don Garrett Jr.)*

A simultaneous project to install the Packard-built Merlin in a Mustang airframe was conducted at North American Aviation in California. NAA Test Pilot Bob Chilton made the first flight in the XP-51B on 30 November 1942. *(AFM)*

"Dutch" Kindelberger beside one of his brand new offspring. *(NAA)*

Rolls-Royce and Packard Motor Car Company in Detroit. Packard production of the Merlin engine began in September 1940. It was officially known as the Packard Merlin 28, and corresponded to the Rolls-Royce-built Merlin Mk. XX. Packard engineers made several changes in the engine for increased reliability such as replacing the copper main bearings with Indium-plated lead main bearings, and nickel-chromium plating of both the intake and exhaust valves for greater heat resistance. Packard also opted to use a new Wright Engine Co. supercharger drive. The finished engine carried the AAF designation V-1650-3. This was the engine that would power the production versions of the Merlin-engine Mustang.

The combination of Merlin engine and Mustang airframe was developed simultaneously on both sides of the Atlantic. As early as May 1942 Rolls-Royce had suggested such a conversion. By June the conversion program was well underway although official studies on the installation were not ready until 14 July. The installation of the Merlin engine into a P-51 airframe was no easy accomplishment. This wasn't your basic bolt a Chevrolet small-block V-8

into a 32 Ford and drive it away! The first thing that had to be done was to make some essential comparative measurements and calculations; the Merlin was about five inches taller than the Allison and 3/4 inch wider; the Merlin engine required a coolant radiator a full 1/3rd larger than the Allison; the oil cooler was somewhat smaller; and the Merlin used an updraft carburetor where the Allison had a down-draft system. The carburetor change meant that the air scoop atop the nose would be empty. Original thinking would have put the intercooler radiator in the vacated carburetor air scoop. However, pilot complaints about the blind spot created by the scoop surfaced and Rolls-Royce engineers moved the intercooler below the engine with the fuel cooler. At this time Rolls-Royce engineers also modified the engine thrust line (i.e., the propeller shaft centerline, raising it 3 1/2 inches). Along with raising the engine, Rolls-Royce engineers also designed a completely new engine mount.

On 12 August 1942, Rolls-Royce began conversion of the first aircraft, Mustang I AL 975. A total of five aircraft were modified (AL 975 & 963, AM 203, 208, and 121) and designated MUSTANG X. Prior to the first flight, the Merlin 61 engine was modified to use a new reduction gear in the two stage supercharger with a new Bendix pressure injection carburetor. The new engine was designated the Merlin 65. Along with the engine changes, a new 10'9"

Jablo propeller from a Spitfire IX was fitted to the Mustang X. On 13 October 1942, RAF Captain Ron Shepard took AL 975 into the air for the first time. The first flight was cut short when the engine cowl came loose, forcing Shepard to land. Later that same day, with the engine cowl firmly attached, Shepard made several passes in excess of 390 mph. On 21 October, the Mustang X was fitted with a new 11'4" prop that had been specifically designed for the Mustang X. The results were an amazing 432 mph at 22,000ft.

In California at almost exactly the same time, North American engineers were working on the same project – installation of a Packard-built Merlin V-1650-3 into a P-51 airframe. On 25 July 1942, North American received authorization to modify two P-51 airframes to accept the Packard-built Merlin engine. Again, as with the Rolls-Royce installation, the upper carburetor air scoop was deleted, and the main engine frame rails were widened and strengthened. The engine thrust line was raised, and the necessary accessories were mounted either under the engine or around the main coolant radiator. It was such a radical conversion that it took some 223,000 engineering hours to accomplish it. It is noteworthy here that it took NAA engineers and craftsmen only 78,000 hours to build the original NA-73X prototype from nothing! It was also so radical that US Army officials deemed the aircraft a totally new design and designated it as the XP-78. This designation was dropped during the actual conversion of the first airframe and P-51 #41-37352 became the XP-51B. The final touch was installation of a Hamilton Standard four blade propeller with propeller "cuffs" for greater efficiency.

After six weeks the XP-51B was complete. Ground tests revealed an overheating problem but engineers were satisfied that a thorough flush of the Glycol system would cure the problem. It didn't! On 30 November 1942, NAA test pilot Bob Chilton took the XP-51B into the air for the first time. He landed 45 minutes later streaming smoke and steam. The radiator was once again clogged and the engine had overheated. The problem was an incompatibility of engine and cooling system metals with Glycol. A new larger Harrison radiator was installed and the radiator air scoop was redesigned. Testing resumed in December 1942 and Bob Chilton soon had the North American-built Merlin Mustang showing a top speed of 447 mph at 30,000 ft., easily 100 mph faster than the Allison-engine Mustangs at the same altitude.

The Rolls-Royce and NAA projections on the performance of the Merlin Mustang led to a letter contract on 26 August 1942 from US Army to North American calling for the production of 400 P-51B aircraft, a full six weeks prior to the first flight of the Mustang X, and 12 weeks before that of the XP-51B. Noise and vibration problems led to multiple design changes in the radiator coolant scoop. The final design saw not only the exterior shape of the scoop change, but also the internal arrangement. Instead of a central radiator body that incorporated both

Brand new Mustang IIIs on the ramp at Mines Field, now LAX, wearing RAF camouflage and serials but with US national insignia for acceptance and test flights. The large camouflage net covered the entire NAA Inglewood production facility! *(NAA)*

P-51C on the line in Texas. The P-51C was simply a P-51B built at the NAA plant in Dallas, Texas. Women made up a very large portion of the aircraft industry work force, and were commonly referred to as "Rosie The Riveter." *(NAA)*

Mustangs and Thunderbolts went to combat theaters aboard cargo ships, tankers, and US Navy aircraft carriers. These P-51Bs being off-loaded at Belfast, Ireland, are the first P-51Bs to arrive in Europe. *(USAF)*

The first AAF group operational in the P-51B was the 354th FG at Boxted in November 1943. This 353rd FS P-51B is being checked out by bomber crews from the 401st BG at Deenethorpe. *(USAF)*

coolant and intercooler radiators, the intercooler radiator was moved forward in the redesigned air scoop housing. The coolant radiator remained in place. The scoop opening was redesigned with a sharply angled inlet that guided the boundary layer air through the radiators, each of which also had its own exit door. Tests of these radiator and scoop designs were conducted on the first XP-51B in the NACA wind tunnel at Ames Aeronautical Laboratory. Although the second XP-51B retained its four 20mm cannon armament as originally required on the P-51, the P-51B production aircraft carried only four .50 caliber machine guns as on the P-51A. In addition, the underwing bomb/drop tank racks were fitted on production aircraft.

The first flight of a production P-51B took place on 5 May 1943. The Inglewood North American facility soon found itself inundated with orders – far more orders than the factory space would allow. Already under production were the Allison-engine Mustang, the AT-6 Texan trainer, and the B-25 Mitchell medium bomber. Now came an order for 400 P-51B Mustangs for USAAF, and 1000 Mustang IIIs for the RAF. North American had a factory in Dallas, Texas that was license-building B-24 Liberators at the time. Army and North American decided to build both AT-6 Texan/Harvard trainers and P-51B Mustangs at the

Dallas plant. Dallas-built aircraft would be designated P-51C, although they were identical to the Inglewood-built aircraft. The Dallas line was modified and the first flight of a Dallas-built P-51C took place on 5 August 1943. Total production was 1988 P-51Bs and 1750 P-51Cs.

There were two important modifications to the P-51B/C during the production run. The Packard Merlin V-1650-7 engine was installed beginning with the P-51B-15 and P-51C-10. The V-1650-7 had a modified supercharger gear reduction ratio that offered an additional 175 hp at 20,000 ft. Secondly, an extra 85 gallon fuel tank was fit into the rear cockpit area above the coolant radiator. This brought the total fuel capacity to 419 gallons with two 75 gallon underwing drop tanks. Colonel Mark Bradley took the first P-51B on its maiden flight from LA to Albuquerque, New Mexico and back to LA. A flight equal to London to Berlin and back! The Allies now had a fighter aircraft to escort the bomber force anywhere in Germany. Although a great many men would still die in World War II, the death knell for Hitler's Thousand Year Reich was beginning to toll.

With production at Inglewood and Dallas well underway, the first P-51Bs were rushed into the combat arena of Europe. The most urgent need was in England

Vance Breese at the controls of the NA-73X Mustang prototype in early November 1940. *(NAA)*

One of the prototype XP-51s survived the war, was restored to flying condition and displayed at the 1976 Oshkosh Fly-In. *(Merle Olmsted)*

A P-51A from an Orlando, Florida AAF training squadron showing heavy exhaust staining during early 1944. *(USAF)*

A 20mm cannon-armed P-51 over Southern California in 1942. *(NAA)*

A P-51A and the XP-51B share the ramp at Mines Field, home of North American Aviation, in late 1943. *(NAA)*

USAAF P-51Bs and RAF Mustang IIIs on line at North American's Inglewood plant in early 1944. Note that the "new" RAF camouflage paint has already weathered badly. *(NAA)*

Above: An RAF Mustang III is captured during its acceptance flight over Mines Field in early 1944. Some RAF Mustang IIIs were delivered in Dark Earth and Dark Green camouflage. *(NAA)*

A USAAF P-51A wears RAF Dark Earth and Dark Green camouflage during a test flight near Los Angeles in early 1942. *(NAA)*

Captains John Godfrey and Don Gentile stand beside Gentiles 4th FG P-51B "Shangri-La." *(USAF)*

"Miss Ruth" leads a flight of 4th FS P-51Ds back from another mission into Germany to their home base at Madna, Italy in 1944. *(USAF)*

A lineup of 23rd FG P-51Ks on the ramp at Hsien, China in 1945. The 23rd FG evolved from the Flying Tigers. *(George McKay)*

"Tika IV" was flown by Lt. Vernon Richards in the 374th FS/361st FG. Lt. Richards is officially credited with 2 air and 4 ground victories. *(USAF)*

Major Pierce McKennon taxis his aircraft, WD-A to the active runway at Debden in 1944. The underwing drop tanks are 110 gallon pressed paper tanks. *(USAF)*

Sgt. Larry Hendle on the wing of "Jan", the 334th FS/ 4th FG P-51D that he crewed at Debden in 1945. *(Larry Hendle)*

The 375th FS has often been said to have Medium Blue camouflage on the upper surfaces of their Mustangs. This photo clearly shows the camouflage to be Olive Drab. *(USAF)*

A P-51D from the 11th FG, Chinese Air Force, on the ramp at Hsien, China in 1945. Mustangs were supplied to the CAF under Lend Lease. *(George McKay)*

Captain John Voll scored 21 victories with the 308th FS/31st FG in "American Maid." Captain Voll shot down five on 16 November 1944. *(USAF)*

"Johnetta IV" was a 336th FS/4th FG P-51D assigned to Lt. Douglas Groshong at Debden in 1945. *(AFM)*

The 3rd Air Commando Squadron flew top cover (escort) missions for 20th AF B-29s attacking the Japanese home islands. They were based on Ie Shima. *(Paul Vercammen)*

A very colorful F-51D from the 57th FG based at Luke AFB in 1949. *(NGB via David Menard)*

This early P-51K from the 376th FS/361st FG carries 75 gallon drop tanks and still has the overpainted remnants of the D-Day bands in July 1944. *(USAF)*

"Tornado", an F-51D from the 40th FS/35th FG assigned to the Occupation Forces in Japan, was based at Irumagawa AB in 1948. *(JEM Aviation Slides)*

Major John England, with 17 1/2 victories in World War II, led "The Red Devils" Mustang demonstration team at Las Vegas AFB (now Nellis AFB) in 1950. *(Colonel Don Gravenstine)*

"Miss Manooky" was one of the F-51Ds supplied to the fledgling Republic Of Korea Air Force under Project BOUT ONE. Although assigned to the ROKAF, they had US pilots commanded by Major Dean Hess, USAF. *(Harry Christman)*

"Promiscuous Miss" and "Sweet Lavonne", a pair of F-51Ds from the 40th FIS/35th FIG at Johnson AB, Japan in 1950. The 35th FIG switched from F-80Cs back to F-51Ds during the early Korean operations. *(Walt Bryan)*

A pair of 500 lb bombs are being loaded on the wing pylons of "Dottie", an F-51D from the 67th FBS/18th FBG at Taegu in 1951. *(USAF)*

"Sooner Snooper" and three other RF-51Ds from the 45th TRS/67th TRG on the ramp at Kimpo in 1952. Known as the "Polka Dots", the 45th TRS flew both RF-51Ds and RF-80s in Korea. *(Major General S.F. Newman)*

Lt. Dick Kempthorne prepares to taxi "Vendetta" back to the parking ramp at Chinhae, K-10, in 1952. "Vendetta" and Lt. Kempthorne were assigned to the shark-mouthed 12th FBS/18th FBG. *(Dick Kempthorne)*

"Miss Marunouchi", a 2 Squadron, SAAF F-51D, pulls onto the active runway at K-10 in 1952 with a full load of 500 lb. bombs and 5" rockets. 2 Squadron aircraft flew deep interdiction raids against the North Korean Reds. *(USAF)*

"Oh-Kaye Baby", an RF-51D from the 45th TRS at Kimpo in 1952. The RF-51Ds flew high speed, low level reconnaissance of the front line positions and over the North Korean road networks. *(Major General S.F. Newman)*

"Dreamboat II", an F-51D from the 39th FBS/18th FBG in 1951. The 39th FS was assigned to three different units and missions in Korea – the 35th FBG, 18th FBG, and finally to the Sabre-equipped 51st FIW at Suwon. *(USAF)*

This F-51D was the personal aircraft of Colonel William Clark, CO of the 18th FBG at K-10 in 1952. Note that the last color band on the fuselage is orange, white, and blue representing 2 Squadron, SAAF, which was assigned to the 18th FBG. *(David Bickel)*

A New Mexico ANG pilot completes the preflight check list before taking off on a practice bombing mission from Kirtland AFB in 1947. Many Guard units painted the state symbol on the fuselage side in place of the national insignia. *(David Menard)*

An F-51D from the 162nd FIS/Ohio ANG at Cox Airport in the early 1950s. The Ohio ANG transitioned to F-84E Thunderjets in 1955. *(Joe Michaels)*

Although the P-51 was a relatively simple aircraft to fly, new pilots learned the controls in "Captive-Air" aircraft such as this P-51C at Orlando Field in 1944. *(Don Garrett Jr.)*

The RAF began receiving Mustang IIIs in December 1943. Although designed for the long range escort mission, most RAF Mustangs served in the fighter-bomber role like this 112 Squadron Mustang III at Tantarella, Italy in 1944. *(via R.L. Ward)*

for use as escort to the 8th Air Force daylight bombing campaign. In September 1943, the first aircraft arrived in England aboard cargo ships. On 11 November 1943, following de-cocooning and re-assembly, the brand new P-51Bs were flown to Boxted where a new unit, the 354th Fighter Group, was being established. The 354th FG/9th Air Force would be the first combat operational Merlin Mustang unit. 9th Air Force? The 9th AF was slated for the ground support mission in Operation OVERLORD, not bomber escort! But the bomber generals at 8th AF Headquarters knew WHY the Mustang was in England. And it wasn't dive-bombing! The 354th FG was soon attached to 8th AF for the bomber escort mission. By December 1943 the training phase was finished for the air and ground crews of the 354th FG, the Pioneer Mustang Group.

On 1 December 1943, the first combat mission was scheduled. It was a fighter sweep over the Pas de Calais area across the Channel. It was actually more a combat familiarization flight than an actual fighter sweep. Leading the 354th FG was the veteran combat leader from the 4th FG, Colonel Donald Blakeslee. The 4th was based at

Debden and equipped with Republic P-47D Thunderbolts. Blakeslee took a quick course on the flight characteristics of the Mustang and was very enthusiastic about the aircraft after his first hop. On 1 December, Blakeslee led six flights of 354th FG Mustangs into France, returning 1 1/2 hours later. No enemy aircraft were sighted. Sadly, Blakeslee had to turn back his new Mustang love and return to the Thunderbolts. However, he did persuade 8th AF to equip the 4th FG with P-51Bs as soon as possible. On 5 December the 354th flew their first bomber escort mission to Amiens, France – again with no enemy aircraft sighted.

The escort mission to Kiel, Germany on 13 December was a different story. It would be 500 miles to the target and back, the longest fighter mission of the war to that date. This time the Luftwaffe did come up to play and Lt. Glenn Eagleston scored a probable victory over a German Messerschmitt Bf 110 twin-engine fighter/bomber. But the Group also lost their first aircraft and pilot. The mission to Bremen on 16 December saw the Groups first victory when Lt. Charles Gumm shot down another Bf

110. The German twin-engine fighter was making a rocket-firing pass on the bomber formation when Lt. Gumm shot it down. It was the first of 701 confirmed aerial victories for the 354th FG, more aerial victories than either the celebrated 4th FG at Debden, or Hub Zemke's 56th FG at Boxted. The 354th Pioneer Mustang Group was the highest scoring air to air Group of the war.

Following the initial batch of P-51Bs into Great Britain were the first production Mustang IIIs for the RAF. No. 19 Squadron at Ford was the first RAF unit to be equipped with the new fighter, being re-equipped and combat operational in Feb 1944. Complaints from both the 354th FG pilots and RAF crews centered about two items – gun jamming and cockpit vision. While the gun-jamming woes would really not be solved until the production of the P-51D, the canopy vision problem was handled by a British engineer, Mr. Robert Malcomb. The pilot complaints centered around the framed canopy of the Mustang. It had many blind spots and was quite uncomfortable for a tall pilot. Robert Malcomb designed a sliding, clear-view perspex bubble canopy to fit the Mustang cockpit opening. Pilots were very enthusiastic about not only the much better all-round view afforded by the bubble canopy, but also the added headroom. The "Malcomb Hood" was so popular that many USAAF units adopted it for use on their Mustangs as well as the RAF units. Mustang IIIs equipped 18 RAF squadrons, while P-51Bs and Cs dominated all facets of USAAF fighter and fighter-bomber aircraft missions.

The 354th FG flew their first combat mission on 1 December 1943, a combat orientation flight over France. Known as the "Pioneer Mustang Group", the 354th had no experience in Mustangs, having been trained in Bell P-39 Airacobras. (USAF)

"Ding Hao!" was the P-51B flown by Major James Howard (see cover). Major Howard shot down 6 1/2 Japanese fighters while flying P-40s with the Flying Tigers. He was awarded the Congressional Medal Of Honor for driving off a squadron of German Bf 110s attempting to shoot down a lone B-17. *(AFM)*

A 126 Squadron Mustang III on the ramp at Leiston wearing the later camouflage of Medium Sea Grey and Dark Green. Except for RAF radio equipment, RAF Mustang IIIs were identical to, and suffered the same problems as USAAF P-51Bs. *(Merle Olmsted)*

"Typhoon McGoon", a P-51B from the 363rd FS/357th FG over England in 1944. With the 75 gallon drop tanks installed, the range of the P-51B went to over 800 miles - or roughly Berlin and back! *(Fred LePage)*

P-51Bs were rushed to bases in the CBI Theater in early 1944. This shark-mouthed P-51B is from the 51st FG at Kunming, China in late 1944. *(USAF)*

An RAF Mustang III from 316 Squadron, Polish Air Force contingent, shows 8 victory marks in 1944. Units of the Polish Air Force were assigned throughout Allied units, sometimes in squadron strength. *(via R.L. Ward)*

"Bonnie Lee", a P-51B assigned to the 486th FS/352nd FG, know as the "Blue-Nosed Bastards from Bodney!" *(AFM)*

Lt. Elmer Cater flew this P-51B with the 368th FS/359th FG based at East Wrotham in late 1944. The aircraft shows some damage from flak on the aft fuselage. *(A.C. Chardella)*

Captain Don Gentile scored 3 victories on 8 April 1944 with the 336th FS/4th FG to bring his total to 15.83. The 4th FG evolved from the American Eagle Squadrons that flew with the RAF in the Battle of Britain in 1940. *(USAF)*

"Killer" was the P-51B flown by Captain Bob Stephens with the 355th FS/354th FG. The white bands around the wings were a quick combat ID marking. *(USAF)*

Lt. R.O. Peters, a 358th FS pilot executed a perfect wheels-up landing at Honnington on 18 July 1944 after German flak holed the radiator and hydraulics. The upper surface D-Day stripes were overpainted in July 1944. *(USAF)*

Colonel "Tex" Hill climbs into the cockpit of his 23rd FG P-51C prior to a mission in October 1944. Hill scored 12 1/4 victories with the Flying Tigers in P-40 Warhawks, adding another 6 Japanese aircraft after the US entered the war. *(USAF)*

"Hot Pants", a 370th FS/359th FG P-51B flown by Lt. Richard Rabb was forced down in Sweden, shows 12 victories under the windscreen. *(via A.C. Chardella)*

Colonel John Meyer flew this P-51C with the 487th FS/352nd FG. The aircraft carries 20 victory marks and has a bar under the code letter indicating the second aircraft in the squadron with the letter "M." *(Don Garrett Jr.)*

"Dakota Kid", a P-51C from the 358th FS/355th FG at Steeple Morden in the Spring of 1944. Note the empty 75 gallon drop tanks in the foreground. *(355th FG Assn.)*

"Sit", a yellow tailed P-51C from the 2nd FS/52nd FG at Madna, Italy, was flown by Lt. Emerson in late 1944. Strangely, the 52nd FG was assigned the same code letters as the 4th FG at Debden, England. *(AFM)*

"Satan's Son", an F-6C from the 107th TRS/67th TRG at Gosselies, Belgium in late 1944. The F-6C was a P-51C fitted with cameras in the rear cockpit and under the rear fuselage. *(Paul Miller)*

The 376th FS taxis to the active runway at Botisham for a mission during the D-Day landings of June 1944. All aircraft have the black and white "D-Day bands" painted on all upper and lower surfaces. *(USAF)*

"Easy Rocking Mama", a 353rd FS/354th FG P-51C flown by Lt. James Burke is covered by camouflage netting at Lashenden in late Spring 1944. By April 1944, most USAAF aircraft were being delivered in natural metal finish without camouflage. *(USAF)*

Major Herschel Green climbs into the cockpit of his P-51B from the black and yellow checker tailed 325th FG at Lesina, Italy. Major Green scored 18 victories with the "Checkertail Clan." *(Don Garrett Jr.)*

This F-6C from the 111th TRS/68th TRG based at St. Raphael, France, has both the Malcomb Hood canopy and a vertical fin fillet added to increase directional stability. *(Don Garrett Jr.)*

This beautifully maintained 353rd FG P-51B was declared "War Weary" and taken out of combat service. It was saved from the scrap heap by these 353rd FG mechanics and used as a "hack" aircraft for VIP flights. *(USAF)*

Surplus P-51Bs and Cs were sold to the general public after the end of World War II for as little as $1000.00. They were flown by ex-military pilots on the pylon racing circuit. *(Don Garrett Jr.)*

The legendary Paul Mantz flew this modified P-51B to wins in the Bendix Trophy Race in 1946, 1947, and 1948, winning over $125,000.00. *(Don Garrett Jr.)*

NORTH AMERICAN AVIATION, INC.
PHOTOGRAPHIC DEPARTMENT
INGLEWOOD CALIFORNIA

Bubble Top - P-51D/K

The P-51D is considered by many to be the ultimate Mustang – that would not come until production of the P-51H. However, most of the problems of the P-51B/C series were ironed out in the P-51D, which ultimately led to its being the best all-round fighter aircraft in World War II. The three main areas of concern were armament, underwing ordnance, and pilot vision. The armament of the P-51B/C series was considered light when compared with contemporary Allied aircraft and, more importantly, the Axis fighters that Mustang pilots had to face. Both the Messerschmitt Bf 109 and Focke-Wulf Fw 190 series had 20mm cannon, with the later jet-powered Messerschmitt Me 262 being armed with 30mm cannon. The gun layout in the Mustang, with the .50 caliber machine guns laying on their sides, led to a great many embarrassing and frightening gun jamming incidents.

North American engineers added another .50 caliber machine gun to each wing, bringing the total to six .50 caliber machine guns. Plenty of punch for any combat, but still not matching the 20mm cannon armament. Additionally, the guns were rearranged and mounted in the gun bays in a vertical position, which brought the ammunition feed chutes in line with the gun breeches. With heated gun bays and the new vertical gun layout, jamming was virtually eliminated. And the added firepower was greatly appreciated by the pilots. Along with the increase in firepower, North American equipped the P-51Ds with an updated gunsight, first the N-9 and later the K-14 gyro gunsight. The underwing ordnance racks and attachment points were strengthened to carry either a pair of 1000 lb. bombs or two drop tanks capable of up to 165 gallons of additional fuel.

The pilot vision problem was a little tougher to solve. The sliding bubble canopy developed by Robert Malcomb for the P-51B/C gave a much better field of vision to the rear and was more comfortable for the taller pilots. But rearward vision was still greatly impaired by the razorback fuselage. What was needed was elimination of the fuselage razorback and adding a full bubble canopy with no impairments such as framing. Plastic research conducted during the design of the Boeing B-17F and Martin B-26B was acquired by North American and used to design and construct a teardrop shape, full bubble canopy with 360 degree vision. A P-51B, #43-12102, was pulled from the assembly line to have the canopy modification performed. The fuselage formers from the windscreen back to the vertical tail were cut down on the top, bringing them level with the top of the engine cowl panel. The new blown bubble canopy was installed on a sliding track, mating up

At this stage all hydraulic and electrical connections are made. Note the silver-painted upper wing and temporary national insignia application. *(NAA)*

The wind tunnel test model for the P-51D canopy modification. *(NAA)*

to a redesigned windscreen. All new fuselage panels were formed to fit the cut down upper rear fuselage. The pilot now had unrestricted vision in all directions, with much greater headroom than any previous model.

Along with the canopy and armament changes, there were several minor modifications that added to the Mustang's already superb overall performance. Small airflow "fences" were added to the upper and lower wings to smooth the airflow over the ailerons. The ailerons were improved in the hinge area to lighten the control loads. Another modification to lighten the wing load was to increase the wing root chord by "kinking" the wing leading edge where it joined the fuselage. Finally, the landing gear was strengthened to handle the increased weight of the additional armament and underwing ordnance. The main wheel bays and doors were also changed. The modified P-51B, now designated XP-51D, made its first flight on 17 November 1943.

Several changes occurred within the P-51D production run including the addition of a fillet in front of the vertical fin to offset a loss of directional stability caused by the removal of the upper fuselage. However, the biggest change occurred within the Dallas production line, resulting in a separate variant – the P-51K. The P-51K was not simply a Dallas-built P-51D. The P-51K had a couple of items that no other Mustang had. The P-51K bubble canopy was a product of the Dallas design team, and was a slightly different shape that offered still more headroom for the pilots. And the P-51K used an Aeroproducts propeller in place of the regular Hamilton Standard prop used on all other Mustang variants. Logistics was the cause for this change. Hamilton Standard could simply not meet the production needs of both the Inglewood and Dallas Mustang plants, plus supply propellers for other types of aircraft such as the Republic P-47 Thunderbolt. An Aeroproducts hollow steel propeller was chosen for the P-51K. However, the Aeroproducts prop suffered a quality control problem with almost 20% being rejected for excessive vibration.

As with all previous Mustang variants, a number of

both the P-51Ds and the P-51Ks were modified on the production line for the photo reconnaissance mission. These aircraft were designated F-6D and F-6K. Three cameras were fitted; a K-17 and K-22 were mounted in the left side of the rear fuselage for oblique photography, and a K-24 vertical camera was mounted in the bottom of the rear fuselage just forward of the tail wheel. Later production aircraft, most of which were slated for service in the Pacific and CBI Theaters, had a direction-finding (DF) loop antenna mounted atop the rear fuselage in a football-shaped housing. F-6D production totaled 136 aircraft, while F-6Ks numbered 163. Both variants would later be redesignated RF-51D and K in the post-war US Air Force era.

The improved Mustang P-51Ds were rushed to the combat theaters in 1944. The first group to receive the P-51D was again the "Pioneer Mustang Group", the 354th FG. But they certainly weren't the last! By the end of 1944 the entire 8th AF, with one exception, was equipped with Mustangs. The exception being, of course, the 56th FG who doggedly held onto their P-47 Thunderbolts through the end of the war. Support units such as the 9th AF, had a mixed bag of Thunderbolts and Mustangs in the fighter-bomber role. The Pacific Theater, with the vast distances between bases and targets, virtually required that groups fly Mustangs, although the Lockheed P-38 Lightning held its own in that war theater.

But the handwriting was on the wall. Following the end of hostilities, all the other fighter types were quickly phased out of service and into the hands of the scrap dealers. It was the Mustang that equipped the post-war Allied air forces. At least until jet fighters could be brought into the inventories. But until such time as jet aircraft were available, it was the P-51D and P-51H that defended the Free World from aggression. And even after the jets were proven and in service, the Mustangs were still needed. As jets became available and units transitioned out of the Mustangs, the P-51s were phased into Air National Guard units, where they served with distinction well into the 1950s.

When the Korean War broke out in June 1950, the Air Force had to bring the Mustang back. The jet fighters were great – very fast, packed a heck of a wallop, and could carry quite a bit of ordnance. But they had one very big problem. They simply had no range. And no range meant very short "loiter time" over the target. In other words the target had better be ready when the jets came into the area. If not, the jets would usually have to head back to Japan to refuel. The Mustang, with its great fuel consumption rate, could loiter in a target area for hours, long enough for the target to be positively identified and attacked. More than once if necessary! In Korea the mission of the Mustang was that of fighter-bomber. They didn't have the speed necessary to mix it up with the speedy MiG-15. Far East Air Force F-51Ds and RF-51Ds flew fighter-bomber missions in support of the GIs on the ground; flew road interdiction missions against North

Two P-51Bs, 43-12101 and -12102, were pulled from the assembly line and modified with a cut down fuselage spine and fitted with a full bubble canopy. First flight for a D model took place on 17 November 1943 with Bob Chilton at the controls. *(NAA)*

The P-51K was a Dallas-built P-51D, but equipped with an Aeroproducts propeller and slightly different canopy shape. However, Dallas-built aircraft were not all P-51Ks. *(NAA)*

North American Test Pilot Joe Barton stands on the wing of the 10,000th Mustang built, which was signed by all the North American employees that built the aircraft. *(NAA)*

Korean truck traffic, flew low-level recon throughout North Korea, and was the primary defense aircraft on any Search and Rescue mission into North Korea. Many a downed pilot thanked his stars for the F-51Ds that roamed overhead while he waited on the chopper to pick him up. The Mustang performed well in any role asked of it in Korea, just as it had in the "Big War."

Today, for all intent and purpose, the wars are over for the Mustangs. Yes, several are still in service with "banana republic" air forces in Central and South America. But for the most part, the only wars left for the Mustangs are the Hollywood "reel wars", where they will always be the stars that they should be.

P-51Ds began arriving in England in the Spring of 1944 in standard Olive Drab and Grey camouflage. Major Thomas Hays flew "Frenesi", being credited with 8 1/2 victories with the 364th FS/357th FG. *(Tom Hayes via Merle Olmsted)*

"Horse's Itch" was flown by Captain Edwin Hiro with the 363rd FS/ 357th FG. The overpainted D-Day bands are clearly visibly. *(Don Garrett Jr.)*

Major Clarence Anderson's first "Old Crow" showing 13 victories under the cockpit. The white wall tires were not an option on the P-51D. *(Don Garrett Jr.)*

Although P-51Ds were delivered in natural metal finish beginning in the late Spring of 1944, many aircraft were camouflaged at combat bases for D-Day operations. "Jackie" is from the 79th FS/20th FG at Kings Cliffe. *(AFM)*

The highest scoring Mustang ace was Major George Preddy, who scored 26.83 victories with the 487th FS/ 352nd FG. Major Preddy had at least four "Cripes A' Mighty" aircraft. *(AFM)*

Major James Goodson exhibits 30 victories and complete D-Day striping on the Debden ramp in June 1944. *(AFM)*

This colorful F-51D was used as a target tug by the 165th FIS/Kentucky ANG at the Air Guard Gunnery Meet held at Gowen Field, Idaho in October 1954. *(P. Paulsen)*

A factory-built TF-51D two-seat fighter-trainer assigned to the 179th FIS/ Minnesota ANG at Duluth. Only 25 aircraft were factory modified to TP or TF-51D configuration. *(Roger Besecker)*

The Air Force Museum aircraft which was stripped and completely refurbished in 1979, finally being painted in the correct World War II paint scheme of "Shimmy IV" flown by Colonel Chet Sluder with the 325th FG in Italy. *(David Menard)*

Colonel Gene Stocker with the Confederate Air Force painted his Mustang as a replica of the aircraft flown by George Preddy, highest scoring Mustang ace during World War II. *(Dick Starinchak)*

"Ge Ge II" is one of the many Mustangs that were converted to pylon racer after the war. Modifications often include clipped wingtips and cut-down canopies which could add up to 50 mph to the top speed. *(Bruce Trombecky)*

One of the most colorful civil Mustangs is "Miss Kat Brat." On this day in September 1979, she was flown by the great Bob Hoover during an airshow at Latrobe, Pennsylvania. *(Dick Starinchak)*

These well maintained F-51Ds from the 179th FIS/Minnesota ANG line the ramp at Duluth in 1954. Note the "0" at the beginning of the serial indicating the aircraft have been in service over 10 years. *(John Dienst)*

Following the quelling of the 1965 uprising in the Dominican Republic, the Dominican Air Force was equipped with even more F-51Ds, but now painted in a jungle-style camouflage of Green and Brown. *(USAF)*

"Dolly" is painted as an aircraft from the 55th FS from the 20th FG at Kings Cliffe in World War II. The aircraft is owned by Bill Clark. *(Dick Starinchak)*

One of the scant few high-performance fixed-wing aircraft remaining in the US Army inventory were several TF-51Ds used as chase aircraft in the Cheyenne helicopter program. *(Mick Roth)*

Possibly the most famous civil Mustang is the one flown by Bob Hoover, official representative for Rockwell International – parent company for North American Aviation. *(Mick Roth)*

"Cloud Dancer", an F-51D converted to a two seater and painted as an RAF Mustang IV. *(Bruce Trombecky)*

P-51Hs from the 61st FS/56th FG share the ramp with the first P-80 Shooting Stars to arrive at Selfridge in late 1946. *(Frank Bueneman)*

This F-51H was assigned to Headquarters Command at Bolling AFB in 1949. It was used as a personal "hack" and demonstration aircraft for airshows in the late 1940s. *(Military Aircraft Slides)*

A pair of New York ANG F-51Hs on the ramp at Gowen Field during the ANG Gunnery Meet in 1954. *(USAF)*

"Midnight Sinner", an F-82G from the 4th Fighter (All-Weather) Squadron over Seoul, Korea in the Summer of 1950.
(Don Garrett Jr.)

A colorful F-51H from the 188th FIS/New Mexico ANG at its home base of Kirtland AFB in the early 1950s.
(Dick Starinchak)

"Our Lil' Lass" was one of the 339th F(AW)S F-82Gs that flew the first missions of the Korean War on 27 June 1950. *(Merle Olmsted)*

"Siamese Lady", a 68th F(AW)S F-82G on the ramp at Itazuke AB, Japan in 1951. The 68th F(AW)S converted to F-94B Starfire jets in the Summer of 1951.

"Miss Guided Virgin" was flown by Lt. D. Allred when he was a flight commander in the 4th F(AW)S at Naha AB, Okinawa in 1950. *(D. Allred)*

"Fool's Paradise IV" from the 380th FS/363rd FG, flew fighter bomber missions in support of the ground troops from advance strips quickly laid down in the hedgerow country of northern France in July 1944. *(USAF)*

"Tempus Fugit", a 308th FS P-51D, shows all of Colonel William Daniel's victories on the fuselage. The 31st FG was based at Foggia Main Field, Italy, in 1945. *(Stan Staples)*

"Patty IV" flown by Lt. Lawrence McCarthy with the 328th FS/352nd FG, the "Blue-Nosed Bastards of Bodney." McCarthy's aircraft shows three victories. *(Don Garrett Jr.)*

A Mustang IV (P-51K) flown by Squadron Leader A. Cox from RAAF 84 Squadron, over Horne Island in 1945. The distinctive canopy shape of the P-51K is readily noted. *(F. Smith via R.L. Ward)*

Lt. Colonel Richard Turner leans on the latest of many "Shortfuse" Mustangs that he flew with the 356th FS/354th FG. Lt. Colonel Turner was credited with 11 German fighter victories. *(Richard Turner)*

"Rolla" was flown by Lt. Ed Hyman in the 362nd FS/357th FG at Leiston in early 1945. Lt. Hyman is credited with two victories. *(Don Garrett Jr.)*

The other modification that made the P-51D was the addition of another .50 caliber machine gun in each wing, plus mounting all the guns vertically to eliminate the jamming that plagued the previous models. *(NAA)*

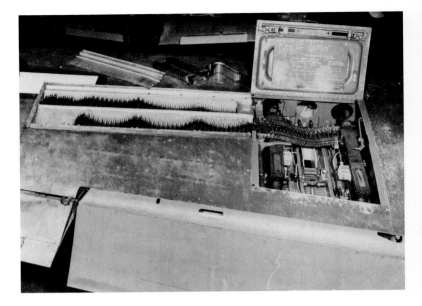

The firewall is installed to the cockpit portion of the fuselage assembly. Instruments and side consoles are also mounted here. *(NAA)*

The coolant radiator is next to be installed. *(NAA)*

Engines are assembled and mounted in the engine cradle, which is then bolted to the fuselage assembly. *(NAA)*

The vertical and horizontal tail empennage is assembled separately (*bottom photo*), then fitted to the fuselage/engine assembly (*above*). *(NAA)*

The wing assemblies are constructed complete with self-sealing fuel cells, landing gear, and ailerons. The wing surfaces, upper and lower, are painted zinc chromate primer before being lacquered in silver. *(NAA)*

Flaps, hydraulics, landing gear doors, and machine guns are installed next. *(NAA)*

Finally the fuselage is brought by crane and assembled to the wing structure. *(NAA)*

Following rollout, all aircraft are put through a series of ground tests on engines, hydraulics, and weapons before flight tests can begin. *(NAA)*

P-51Ks stand ready for delivery to New Zealand, Australian, US Army Air Force, and Royal Air Forces beside a Lend-Lease AT-6 Texan bound for the Soviet Air Force. *(NAA)*

The K-14 gunsight as mounted in later model P-51Ds. Note that the correct wingspan is obtained by "dialing in" the aircraft type. *(NAA)*

The 2nd FS/52nd FG are lined up on the PSP ramp at Madna, Italy in 1945. The 52nd FG flew escort for 15th AF B-17s and B-24s going to targets in Germany, Italy, and the occupied Balkans nations. *(AFM)*

"Jersey Bounce" was Lt. Vic Iglesias' aircraft when he served with the 357th FS/355th FG at Steeple Morden in early 1945. *(Don Garrett Jr.)*

Artwork on Mustangs was never as prevalent as on P-47s and P-38s, usually only having a nickname. However, the exceptions could be superb such as Captain Charles Weaver's P-51D. Captain Weaver shot down 8 enemy aircraft with the 362nd FS/357th FG. *(Merle Olmsted)*

"Betty-E" was the personal aircraft of Lt. Colonel Wayne Blickenstaff with the black and yellow checker-nosed 350th FS/353rd FG at Raydon. Lt. Colonel Blickenstaff scored 10 victories, including 5 on the 24 March 1945 mission. *(via Merle Olmsted)*

"Billy Boy," a 383rd FS/364th FG P-51D returning to home base at Honnington in late 1944 following another 8th AF mission deep into Germany. *(Don Garrett Jr.)*

"Bergie III/Pride And Joy" was flown by Lt. William Hess with the 384th FS/364th FG at Honington in December 1944. Lt. Hess scored 3 victories. *(USAF)*

"Ridge Runner" showing the full markings and 20 victories, was the personal aircraft of Major Pierce McKennon with the 335th FS/4th FG at Debden in 1945. *(Don Garrett Jr.)*

"Libbuf Nanny", flown by Lt. Richard Neece with the 385th FS/364th FG, showing three victories on the canopy rail. *(Don Garrett Jr.)*

"Esie 4" flown by Major Carl Stapleton with the 385th FS/364th FG in late 1944 at 8th AF Station F-375, Honnington. *(USAF)*

"Tar Heel" shows 11 victories for Captain James Starnes with the 504th FS/339th FG based at Fowlmere in early 1945. *(USAF)*

A quartet of F-6D reconnaissance aircraft on the ramp at Speke Airport get their final checks prior to delivery to the 69th TRG at Nancy, France in the Spring of 1945. *(USAF)*

Above: Mustangs were delivered to fighter groups in the Pacific Theater aboard cargo ships and, in this case, US Navy aircraft carriers. *(USAF)*

Above left: "Black's Bird", an Olive Drab camouflaged P-51D assigned to the 79th FS/20th FG at Kings Cliffe in December 1944, mounting 110 gallon pressed paper drop tanks under the wings. *(AFM)*

Left: "Sigh!", a P-51D from the 51st FG at Asanol, India in 1945. The checkertail indicates an aircraft from the 25th FS. *(Don Garrett Jr.)*

The 35th FG is lined up on the parking ramp at Yontan Airfield on Okinawa in July 1945. From Okinawa the Mustangs could roam at will anywhere over the Japanese island empire - or what was left of it! *(USAF)*

Above: "Miss Toopy II" is a P-51K from the 76th FS/23rd FG based at Liuchow, China in 1945. *(George McKay)*

P-51Ks, like this 3 Squadron, RAAF aircraft in the PSP revetment at its base in Italy, were supplied via the Lend Lease authority. *(Don Garrett Jr.)*

"Kiss Me" was flown by Lt. Widger with the 41st FS/35th FG based at Naha, Okinawa in 1945. As soon as Okinawa was secure, Mustangs moved into the captured airfields for missions against the Home Islands. *(Bomber Books)*

Crew Chiefs push a yellow-tailed 462nd FS P-51D back into the dispersal area at one of the airfields on Iwo Jima in July 1945. Iwo was the main base used by B-29 "cripples" coming back from Japanese targets. *(USAF)*

This P-51D was assigned to 9th AF Headquarters when photographed at a Clovis Field airshow in May 1946. The 9th AF was transferred from Europe to Biggs Field, Texas in 1946. *(USAF)*

With jet aircraft being in demand by the combat units fighting in Korea, many air defense units remained equipped with propeller fighters. This pair of F-51Ds is from the 37th FIS at Ethan Allen AFB in October 1953. *(Marty Isham)*

A TP-51D from the 31st FG at Triolo, Italy in late 1945, assigned to Group Headquarters as indicated by the three-color bands on the nose, fuselage, and tail – red, yellow, and blue. *(Allen Troupe via Fred Johnson)*

"Vivian" and "Kathryn" lead this lineup of F-51Ds from the 35th FBG on the snow covered ramp at Chitose AB, Japan in 1949. *(USAF)*

Led by Major Dean Hess, US pilots taught South Korean pilots how to fly and fight in surplus F-51Ds under Project BOUT ONE. The US pilots, however, were often called upon to fly combat missions alongside their Korean "pupils." *(USAF)*

The 12th FBS was one of the four Mustang-equipped squadrons within the 18th FBG at Pyongyang Main Field in October 1950, during the UN push to the Yalu River. Three of the squadrons were USAF, while the fourth was South African Air Force. *(USAF)*

"Sandy" and "Darlin' Joe" sit with other 40th FBS F-51Ds on the ramp at K-16, Seoul City Airport, in May 1951. The aircraft are armed with 5" rockets and napalm bombs. *(US Army)*

A 195th FBS/California ANG F-51D undergoes major engine maintenance in the hangar at Van Nuys Airport in 1953. *(NAA)*

An F-51D from 77 Squadron, Royal Australian Air Force at K-24, near Pyongyang, North Korea in November 1950. 77 Squadron soon converted to Meteor Mk. 7 jets when Soviet-built Mig-15s entered the war. *(USAF)*

Front line reconnaissance missions and North Korean road traffic were monitored by RF-51Ds from the 67th TRG at K-14, Kimpo. "My Peggy" is assigned to the 45th TRS. *(AFM)*

The 35th FIG changed missions and aircraft three times during the Korean War. They started in F-80C Shooting Star jets in the interceptor role, transitioned to F-51D fighter-bombers, and finally obtained F-86F Sabre jets in 1953. *(via Dave McLaren)*

Mustangs equipped many of the Air National Guard units in the late 1940s and into the middle 1950s. These Nevada ANG F-51Ds are assigned to the 192nd FBS based at Reno in 1954. *(Don Garrett Jr.)*

"Ol' Nab Sob", a 67th FBS F-51D, negotiates the puddles at Chinhae. The Korean monsoon left many of the UN airfields flooded and almost unusable. *(USAF)*

A final attempt to bring the Mustang back into action was the Piper Enforcer, an F-51D with a turbo-prop powerplant and wingtip tanks. It would have been used in a Vietnam-style conflict in the counter-insurgency role. *(Tom Brewer)*

"Wham Bam", an F-51D from the 167th FBS/West Virgina ANG flew the last Mustang mission when Major James Little delivered the aircraft to the Air Force Museum at Wright Patterson AFB, Ohio. *(USAF)*

During the Dominican Republic crisis in early 1965, US forces came upon this all-grey Dominican Air Force F-51D at the Santo Domingo Airport. *(USAF)*

Mustangs were supplied to many nations under the Military Assistance Program, including the Philippine Air Force. The 5th FW F-51Ds, based at Manila, flew counter-insurgency strikes against communist rebels in the late 1950s. *(Jun Amper)*

An F-51D from the 107th FIS/ Michigan ANG taxis to its parking spot at Selfridge AFB. F-51Ds were withdrawn from Guard units to keep the combat units in Korea at peak strength. *(Dave McLaren)*

Lightweight - P-51H

There were two more production aircraft in the evolution of the Mustang design – the P-51H lightweight Mustang and the P-82 Twin Mustang. Both were results of Allied needs in World War II, or projected needs. However, neither aircraft would see any combat during World War II. The P-51H would be overshadowed by the coming of the jet age. And while the P-82 would actively serve into the early 1950s and see combat in the Korean War, it too was quickly replaced by jet aircraft.

The object of building a lightweight version of the Mustang was an effort to increase both the rate of roll and the rate of climb, both of which are directly affected by excessive weight. Both the Fw 190 and the Bf 109 fighters that defended the German Reich had roll rates better than the P-51D. And the Japanese fighters, like the Zero and Oscar, had much greater rates of climb. Why? Didn't the Mustang have the most aerodynamic fuselage/wing structure of any piston-engine fighter in the War? Wasn't the Packard-Merlin engine one of the most powerful engines? The answer to both of those questions was Yes – but! The problem was weight. The Mustang with all its armor plate to protect the pilot, self-sealing fuel tanks, guns and ammunition, electrical and hydraulic systems – all of this made the aircraft much heavier than contemporary aircraft.

In 1943 Edgar Schmued began a project to reduce the weight of his prize aircraft design. The projected weight was to be no more than 5700 lbs., down 1300 lbs. from the production P-51D weight of 7000 lbs. The wing was decreased in thickness and the wing root "crank" was eliminated. Since the aircraft was to be lighter, the landing gear did not need to be as strong. More weight savings here. A totally new lightweight landing gear strut, with spot disc brakes and smaller wheels and tires was used. Although the engine would remain the venerable Packard-Merlin V-1650-3, the engine would be mounted in a re-designed engine mount that cut another 100 lbs from the weight. And it would use an all-new lightweight Aeroproducts three blade aluminum propeller. The cooling system was redesigned to incorporate a heat exchanger in place of the oil cooler and coolant lines. All of this was in a redesigned fuselage with a longer coolant radiator scoop under the fuselage and a longer, more streamlined bubble canopy. Finally, the inboard .50 caliber guns were eliminated saving the weight of both guns and ammo feeds. The aircraft was designated XP-51F.

Rollout of the XP-51F came early in 1944 with Bob Chilton making the first flight on 14 February 1944. The

A flight of four 57th FG P-51Hs over the snow-covered Alaskan mountains in 1946. At this time the aircraft still were marked with a WWII-style unit code. (USAF)

The fifth production P-51H illustrates the many differences from the P-51D including different landing gear, reshaped radiator intake, staggered underwing rocket launch stubs, and the much thinner wing. *(NAA)*

results of Schmued's weight reduction program were impressive. The XP-51F empty weight was 5635 lbs., 2000 lbs. less than the P-51D. Combat weight was 9060 lbs., as compared with the P-51Ds combat weight of 11,600 lbs. The rate of climb was 4000 feet/minute compared with 3475 ft/min of the P-51D. Top speed was 466 mph in clean condition. The P-51D top speed was 437 mph. Combat range was reduced to 650 miles since the XP-51F did not have either the rear fuselage fuel tank nor underwing drop tanks. USAAF and British officials were very impressed but did find that the aircraft lacked directional stability due to the use of a standard P-51D vertical tail. A taller tail was needed.

Three of the five experimental lightweight airframes were finished as XP-51Fs or Mustang Vs. The final two airframes, designated XP-51G, would be powered by an experimental Rolls-Royce engine, the RM-14SM, and were to have Rotol five blade propellers. The RM-14SM developed 2080 hp at 20,000 feet through use of the experimental Skinner Union fuel injection system. The XP-51G was slated to have a Rotol five blade, densified wooden propeller as used on the Spitfire Mk. XIV. But the Rotol propeller was not available by rollout and an Aeroproducts four-blade propeller was fitted in its place. The Rotol propeller was evidently fitted to the XP-51G

between the 3rd flight on 10 August and the 4th flight. The Rotol prop was only used on the first XP-51G as test flights revealed that the aircraft was very unstable and Bob Chilton deemed it unsuitable for further tests. Thus the XP-51G test flights were made with the Aeroproducts four-blade propeller installed. When the Skinner injection worked the results were astounding! Test Pilot Ed Virgin took the XP-51G on its maiden flight on 9 August 1944. A top speed of 495 mph was instrumented during an RAF test flight in February 1945 and over 500 mph speeds were reported. The aircraft potentially had a 46,000 ft. service ceiling but the cockpit was not pressurized and test pilots were forced to drop back to a comfortable altitude. Although the performance was phenomenal, the many problems with the experimental engine and fuel injection forced NAA engineers to curtail development.

With the XP-51F and XP-51G test results in hand, NAA engineers settled on a compromise of sorts. They would use the airframe from the XP-51F powered by a later model Packard-Merlin V-1650-9. Packard would guarantee both engine deliveries and engine reliability since the -9 was a further development of a production powerplant. The V-1650-9 was mated to another new Aeroproducts propeller design, the Aeroproducts Unimatic H20D156-23M5. The V-1650-9 with water injection, could

The P-51H could easily carry the Lockheed-designed 165 gallon drop tanks, which extended the ferry range to 2900 miles. *(NAA)*

produce 1930 hp in War Emergency setting. The directional stability problem was overcome by increasing the rear fuselage length thirteen inches and the height of the vertical fin/rudder. The length of the canopy was reduced to that of a standard P-51D/K but the entire cockpit area was raised several inches above the level of the fuselage spine. Projected performance of the now designated P-51H, based on the results of the XP-51F/G tests, brought a June 1944 order from US Army Air Force for 2000 Inglewood-built P-51Hs and 1629 Dallas-built P-51Ms.

Bob Chilton took the first P-51H into the air on 3 February 1945. The prototype and the first 19 production aircraft were all built with the standard P-51D/K short vertical tail/rudder. Beginning with the 20th production aircraft, and retrofitted to all the earlier aircraft, the taller tail was fitted. Several items that had been deleted on the XP-51F were returned on the production P-51H. The inboard .50 caliber machine guns were re-installed for a total of six and an ammunition capacity of 1820 rounds. The fuselage fuel tank was also installed but the fuel capacity was reduced to 50 gallons. This brought internal

fuel capacity to 255 gallons. Provision for carriage of underwing fuel tanks was incorporated.

Test pilots soon had the P-51H establishing all sorts of records including being the fastest production piston-engine airplane in World War II at 487 mph. The ferry range with a pair of 165 gallon drop tanks installed was 2900 miles, while combat range with 110 gallon combat tanks under the wings was 1104 miles – over 100 miles further than the P-51D/K. However, the great performance of the H could not overcome two critical factors upon which its production life hinged – the end of the war and the beginning of the jet age. Of the 3629 P-51H/M aircraft ordered by USAAF in June 1944, Inglewood built only 555 P-51Hs. The Dallas production of the P-51M ended after one aircraft was built, and that aircraft was simply a standard P-51K with the V-1650-9 engine and Hamilton Standard propeller installed.

By the end of World War II in August 1945, there were 370 P-51Hs in service with AAF units, mostly training units in Florida. The only combat operational unit in the P-51H was the 39th Photo Recon Squadron based at March

A rare photo of Ohio ANG F-51Hs from the 162nd FIS on the ramp at Wright Patterson AFB in 1954. The Ohio ANG flew the F-51H only a few months before converting to F-84 Thunderjet fighter-bombers. *(USAF)*

Field, California. They were equipped with 11 P-51Hs and 6 F-6Ds in late-Summer 1945. No P-51Hs made it to front line units anywhere during World War II, although several people claim to have seen them in the Pacific. The P-51H would become the front line aircraft of the post-War Army Air Force, at least until new jet fighters could be brought into the inventory. Veteran units like the 56th Fighter Group at Selfridge Field, 57th FG at Ladd Field, Alaska, and the 82nd FG at Grenier Field, New Hampshire were equipped with P-51Hs until Lockheed P-80 Shooting Star jet fighters became available. The 56th FG and 82nd FG were assigned to Strategic Air Command as Very Long Range Escort Groups. With mass introduction of the Lockheed P-80 Shooting Star, Republic P-84 Thunderjet, and North American F-86 Sabre into Air Force inventories, the (now designated) F-51Hs rapidly phased out of active units into Air National Guard service, equipping no fewer

than 61 ANG squadrons, some having only one F-51H assigned however. The first ANG unit to equip with the F-51H was the 164th FS/Ohio ANG based at Mansfield Lahm Airport in July 1949. The last ANG F-51H mission was flown by another Ohio squadron, the 112th FS based at Akron-Canton Airport.

Ironically, with the outbreak of the Korean War, and the recall to duty of hundreds of combat veteran P-51D/K Mustangs and some 22 ANG units, no F-51Hs saw any combat in that Police Action either. The P-51H/F-51H, although being the fastest, highest-flying, longest ranged Mustang variant produced, was the only type to see no combat duty. Today there are at least five P-51Hs still in existence. Two are museum aircraft at Lackland AFB, Texas and Chanute AFB, Illinois. There are at least three P-51Hs in civilian pilots hands.

One of the first units operational in the P-51H was the 56th FG at Selfridge Field, Michigan in 1946. Ironically, the 56th FG was the only 8th Air Force unit in WWII not to transition to Mustangs. *(Art Krieger)*

As the Air Force rapidly converted to jet aircraft, the P-51Hs were relegated to Air National Guard service such as these aircraft with the District of Columbia's 191st FIS. *(Dave McLaren)*

T/Sgt. Kelley watches the F-86 equipped Sabre Knights Aerobatic Team perform from atop his 194th FIS/California ANG F-51H at an airshow at Hamilton AFB in 1955. *(NAA)*

A mixed flight of New York (#259) and Pennsylvania ANG F-51Hs prepare for a flight from Spaatz Field at Reading, PA in September 1953. The taller tail of the H model is quite evident. *(USAF)*

P-82 Twin Mustang

The P-82 Twin Mustang was a development directly tied to possible future war targets much further from Allied bases than was Berlin. By 1943 thoughts were being given as to what was going to be needed as escort for bomber aircraft enroute to targets on the Japanese Home Islands. The closest Allied bases were at Tinian, Saipan, and in China. It was far outside the range of even the long-legged Merlin Mustang and P-38 Lightning. What was needed was a base much closer to Japan or a longer ranged fighter aircraft. Eventually both were acquired. Bases on Iwo Jima and in mainland China brought Allied fighters within range of even the farthest targets on the Japanese Islands. And North American's engineers came up with the needed range that might have been required had not the Marines went through the hell of capturing Iwo Jima.

Edgar Schmued came up with an idea for mating two Mustang fuselages together, complete with dual-control cockpits so that one pilot could relieve the other on the missions that were projected to be over twelve hours in length. The two fuselages would be joined by a single center wing that would house the armament, and a one piece horizontal tailplane. The fuselage/wing structure chosen was that of the XP-51F with the thin wing and extended fuselage. The wing outer panels, now without any weapons bays, could hold 196 gallons of fuel, with an additional 182 gallons in the center wing. The lightweight fuselage was lengthened 57 inches for greater directional stability. Directional stability was also enhanced by use of a pair of much larger dorsal fin fillets and wider vertical fins. However, the initial XP-82s were completed with standard P-51D vertical tail surfaces.

Power would come from a pair of uprated Packard Merlins, the V-1650-11 and -21, which could produce up to 2270 hp in War Emergency Setting with water injection. The -21 was the same engine as the -11 except that it used a gear reduction box to rotate the propeller in the opposite direction. In March 1944, one year prior to the first flight of the XP-82, Army ordered 500 P-82s from North American based on the proposal. However, as the program advanced it became increasingly obvious that production of the P-82 would probably not take place until after the war had ended. The end of the war would mean that Packard Motor Car Co. would probably return to the automobile business and Merlin engines would therefore have to be purchased from Rolls Royce in England. Not an enjoyable thought to Army planners. Luckily, the

"Betty Jo", one of the 18 P-82Bs produced. "Betty Jo" flew a record flight from Honolulu to New York City – 5051 miles nonstop! All the P-82Bs were assigned to Air Training Command. *(USAF)*

When the XP-82 was rolled out in June 1945, it was configured for a variety of missions, including fighter-bomber with bombs, rockets, and an eight gun pod. *(AFM)*

The fuselage/center wing mockup of the XP-82. The shape of the radar pod was extensively changed on production aircraft. *(NAA)*

Allison engineers had ironed out most of the bugaboos in the V-1710 program and had developed a very reliable, high performance, high altitude engine. Army authorized use of the Allison engine in the P-82 series. The engines slated for the P-82 series were the V-1710-143 and -145, which could also produce 2250 hp.

The first flight of the XP-82 took place on 15 April 1945. The flight tests produced some very enthusiastic results; top speed was 482 mph at 20,000 ft.; range was almost 1400 miles on the internal fuel supply. And this was an aircraft that weighed almost twice that of a combat Mustang. However, World War II ended in August 1945

and brought with it the inevitable cutbacks in defense spending. The production order for P-82B/C/D aircraft was cut from 500 aircraft to 20 — 18 production P-82Bs and one each XP-82C and XP-82D night interceptor aircraft. The entire run of P-82Bs was used in the test or training mission, and no aircraft found their way to a combat unit. The B model did have some fame however when "Betty Jo", a P-82B, demonstrated its long legs to the entire world. Lt.Colonel R.E. Thacker and Lt. J.M. Ard flew the "Betty Joe" from Hickam AFB, Hawaii to New York — nonstop! They covered the 5051 miles at an average speed of 342 mph.

The XP-82C and XP-82D were the first efforts to develop a long range interceptor aircraft. The Northrop P-61 Black Widow was a good aircraft, but certainly no match for a Mustang or a Twin Mustang. The XP-82C was a production P-82B that had a large pod under the center wing that contained an SCR-720C airborne intercept radar unit, the same unit as in the P-61 Black Widow. Although the SCR-720 was a state of the art unit for the era, it was plagued with problems such as image distortion during violent aircraft maneuvers. The radar pod had to extend far out in front of the wing so that the propellers would not cause interference with the radar. The XP-82D was a similar aircraft but used the smaller AN/APS-4 radar as was found on the Lockheed P-38M night fighter. Both aircraft used the second cockpit in the right fuselage as a radar operators station.

The first of the production P-82 Twin Mustangs to be powered by the Allison engines was the P-82E. They were projected to be the extra-long range escort fighter that Strategic Air Command needed to escort the huge Convair B-36 and Boeing B-50 bombers to Soviet targets in the Cold War era. With the exception of the modified exhaust panel and different exhaust stacks, the Allison-powered P-82E looked almost exactly like the Merlin-powered P-82B. For additional firepower, a pod developed along the lines of the radar pod, was fitted with an additional eight .50 caliber machine guns. This pod, however, never went into production and production P-82Es were armed with the internal six .50s only. Underwing attachments were added for carriage of rocket launching "trees" and/or drop tanks. Up to four 300 gallon drop tanks could be carried.

In October 1946, Army issued a contract to North American to build 250 P-82E escort fighters. The delivery of the first aircraft was to take place in November 1946. However, a continuous string of problems set the delivery date of that first aircraft back to April 1947. The biggest problem was the one that Army thought they had avoided by choosing the US-built Allison over the Rolls Royce Merlin – engine availability. It wasn't that Allison couldn't build enough engines, they were simply beset with so many problems (superchargers, spark plug fouling, oil leaks, etc) that the entire P-82 program was almost killed off.

By the end of 1947, the (now) US Air Force had accepted only four F-82Es, and those were restricted to test flights only. North American continued the F-82E assembly line without engines. Unfinished aircraft minus engines, had to be stored at the Convair facility in nearby Downey, CA. until the engines became available. A crash program by North American, USAF, and Allison did correct the problems and production engines started reaching the finished airframes in early 1948. The first production F-82Es reached SACs 27th Fighter Group (VLR) in May 1948, the unit being fully equipped by the end of 1948. By 1951, SAC had no further use for the long range propeller-driven fighter escort and the F-82Es were phased out in favor of F-84E Thunderjets. Besides, SAC was now

Captain Ray Sharpe climbs into the cockpit of "Ole 97", Colonel Cy Wilson's aircraft when he commanded the 27th FG in 1948. *(via Warren Thompson)*

A P-82E from the 523rd FS/27th FG based at McChord AFB in 1948. The 27th FG was the first operational P-82 unit. Note that the aircraft still carries the "P" for Pursuit buzz number. *(AFM)*

"Night Takeoff", an F-82G from the 319th FIS at Moses Lake AFB, Washington in the late 1940s, illustrates that the radar pod could, and was, used other purposes. *(via David Menard)*

equipped with the Boeing B-47 Stratojet bomber, fast enough at the time to run away from the enemy interceptors. The production run of the F-82E stopped after 100 aircraft were built.

The final 150 aircraft on the Twin Mustang contract were completed as F-82F and F-82G all-weather interceptors. The Air Force was somewhat unwilling to go ahead with the all-weather variant as jet interceptors were already being developed. However, the first jet interceptor, the Lockheed F-94 Starfire, would not see squadron service until late 1950. That meant that the air defense of the continental United States would have to be handled by the aging Northrop Black Widows. The Russians had the A-bomb and plenty of B-29 copies to deliver it. The F-82F/G program was given the go-ahead so that a viable, reasonably high performance aircraft was available to the fledgling Air Defense Command.

The all-Black F-82F was an F-82E that was fitted with the underwing radar pod housing the AN/APG-28 tracking radar. The APG-28 was slightly inferior to the SCR-720 series in the search mode, but was a much better unit for the all-weather mission. The F-82F had a full radar operators station in the right cockpit without flight controls. The pilots cockpit had an autopilot and a radar scope added. Deliveries of the first operational F-82Fs began in September 1948 to the 325th FG. By late 1949 both the 52nd FG at Mitchell AFB and the 325th FG at Hamilton AFB were fully equipped. North American built 100 F-82Fs before production was halted. The first F-82Fs were phased out of service in mid-1950 when the first F-94A Starfire jet interceptors came into the inventory.

The F-82G was almost exactly the same aircraft as the F-82F except that it had the SCR-720C search radar in the underwing pod. Again the aircraft was painted all-Gloss Black and it had a full radar operators station in the right cockpit. Performance of the F-82F/G Twin Mustang,

even with the ungainly and heavy radar pod hung under the center wing, rivaled that of its escort fighter cousin the F-82E. Combat range was almost 2000 miles, with a combat speed of 400 mph and a service ceiling over 37,000 feet. Very impressive for a fighter of its size and configuration. Deliveries of the first F-82Gs went to the 68th F(AW)S at Itazuke AB, Japan in 1949. Nine F-82F and five F-82G aircraft were modified for cold weather operations in Alaska and assigned air defense duties with the 449th F(AW)S at Ladd AFB. These aircraft were designated as F-82H. North American built 50 F-82Gs which filled out the Twin Mustang contract. These were the final Mustangs to be produced.

By June 1953 the Air Force had phased out of service all F-82E/F/G/H aircraft. However, before being phased out of service, the F-82G was to play a significant role in President Harry Truman's Korean Police Action. The F-82Gs of the 4th, 339th, and 68th F(AW)Ss based in Japan on that fateful Sunday in June 1950, were the only fighter aircraft in the Far East capable of flying the air defense mission over the evacuation ports in Korea for any reasonable amount of time. The F-80 Shooting Stars flew many missions from their Japanese bases over Seoul and Inchon. But their "loiter time", or amount of time they could stay on station, was only about 10 minutes before they had to begin their return to Japan to refuel. The F-82Gs could remain on station for a couple of hours. On 27 June 1950, a pair of 68th F(AW)S F-82Gs shot down the first two North Korean aircraft of the Korean War. Lt. Wm. Hudson and Carl Fraser (R/O) shot down a Yak-11 and Lts. Charles Moran and Fred Larkins (R/O) shot down a Yak-7, both victories coming over Kimpo AB, west of Seoul. By the end of F-82 operations in Korea in February 1952, 5th AF Twin Mustang crews would claim four air to air and 16 ground victories.

A pair of 68th F(AW)S F-82Gs on the ramp at Kimpo in late 1950. The all-weather capabilities of the F-82G made it the prime night interceptor aircraft until the F-94B Starfire came to Korea in late 1951. *(USAF)*

Crew chiefs work on the big Allison powerplants on this F-82G from the 68th F(AW)S at Ashiya AB, Japan in August 1950. *(USAF)*

Lt. William Hudson, with Lt. Carl Fraser as RO, scored the first "kill" of the Korean War in F-82G #46-383. Lt. Hudson shot down a North Korean Yak fighter over Kimpo on 27 June 1950. *(Merle Olmsted)*

"Lover Boy", an F-82G from the 339th F(AW)S on the ramp at Kadena AB, Okinawa in the Summer of 1950. FEAF F-82Gs were the primary air defense weapon over Korea in the early days of the war. *(Merle Olmsted)*

Colonel Carrol McColpin, CO of the 52nd FG at Mitchell AFB in 1947, leads another 52nd FG F-82F over the New York countryside. The 52nd FG was one of the first groups in the newly established Air Defense Command. *(USAF)*